SCARLET LETTER LIVES

Maureen K. Wlodarczyk

Also by Maureen Wlodarczyk:

Past-Forward:
A Three-Decade and Three-Thousand-Mile Journey
Home

Young & Wicked:
The Death of a Wayward Girl

Canary in a Cage:
The Smith-Bennett Murder Case

Jersey! Then . . . Again

"No man for any considerable period can wear one face to himself and another to the multitude, without finally getting bewildered as to which may be the true one."

~Nathaniel Hawthorne

CONTENTS

PREFACE

It's a story set in Puritan New England in the 17th century . . . written in the mid-19th century.   It's the story of young woman's fall from grace and her strength in the aftermath . . . written with exceptional sensitivity and clarity of insight by a middle-aged man. Its setting and attendant social norms are alien to our world of today . . . yet its timeless themes have resonated with every generation since its author put pen to paper over 160 years ago.   It is an American literary masterpiece . . . it is *The Scarlet Letter* by Nathaniel Hawthorne, first published in 1850.

Decades ago, when I was a college prep high-achiever in high school, "English" was a class I endured rather than enjoyed. History was a favorite of mine but, in my youthful ignorance, I had yet to make the connection that reading classic literature means immersing oneself in a historical journey.   Years later when I turned to audiobooks as companions for my very long commute to work, I "discovered" the classics on my own terms. Since then, I haven't stopped reading and rereading the wonderful works of Jane Austen, the Brontes, George Eliot, Thomas Hardy and their peers, including Nathaniel Hawthorne. Each of these classic books tells a story that transcends the passage of time, changes in societal norms, and prevailing standards of morality. The characters, their predicaments, struggles, decisions, failures, and sometime redemption or triumph are not unique. Whether yesterday or 160 years ago, each of us travels a winding road that marks out his or her own unique life journey. Love, loss, failure, success, and an endless array of surprises await the traveler. The ageless relevance of classic literature lies in the authors' ability to use the vehicle of our ordinary lives to capture the human condition in a way that creates a bond between their characters and we readers. We admire Hawthorne's Hester Prynne while we loathe Roger Chillingworth. We hope for a happy ending and, when there is none, we close the book knowing that our heroine Hester has endured all with amazing dignity, penitentially sacrificing herself for her child and the two men who failed her. How could a theme like that ever be "dated?"

I have an affection for antiquarian books. I am not talking about the rarest and most expensive of old books. I am drawn to owning battle-worn survivors of early editions that were put into circulation when their authors were still living. Some years ago, I purchased an early copy of *The Scarlet Letter* published in 1852. In my mind, I imagined a Victorian-era woman reading the book I now own, her eyes taking in the words as Hawthorne weaves the tale of Hester Prynne. How many pairs of eyes, male and female, moved down and turned those pages, passing that book on until the day it became mine?

Since then, I have purchased two other early copies of *The Scarlet Letter*. Like the first copy I bought these were also published by Ticknor, Reed, and Fields of Boston, one in 1852 and the other in 1853. All three books had something in common beyond Ticknor, Reed, and Fields being the publisher: each had an inscription identifying the former owner of the book. I wondered if those owners were, in fact, the original book owners and that curiosity naturally led to me firing up my genealogical research skills in an attempt to reconnect books and owners.

Eventually, I succeeded in tracking all three copies of *The Scarlet Letter* back to their original owners who, in all three cases, were the people identified in the inscriptions. My genealogical and historical searches for the owners of those 160-year-old books led me south to Virginia, Mississippi, and Louisiana during the decade leading up to the outbreak of the Civil War. From that historical anchor point, I would eventually reach back and then forward in time piecing together the lives of the three people who first opened those books and whose eyes first moved down their pages as Hawthorne drew each of them into the story of a young woman in New England.

Three randomly found copies of *The Scarlet Letter*, one owned by a man, one by a woman, and the third by a boy of thirteen. Two of the books were found in the United States, one of those on Ebay. The third book, its first owner living in Louisiana, was found 160 years later in the far west of Canada. Three books, three lives, each of those lives touched by a work of fiction that is recognized as the first true "American" novel. Each book, inscribed with the original owner's name, carried his or her identity forward in time across more than a century and a half as each moved from owner to owner and place to place until found and acquired by me.

My research efforts have rediscovered their diverse lives and yielded the gamut of personal circumstances, experiences, and fortunes including elements of success, tragedy, bravery, commitment, and resilience. As I learned in doing family history research for so many years, interesting or memorable lives are not synonymous with fame (or infamy). The daily lives of "ordinary" people – including those who made our own lives possible – can fascinate, inspire, enlighten . . . or impart a cautionary tale. Said simply: those lives can resonate generations after they ended. I have taken historical and genealogical aspects of the lives of those three book owners as inspiration, adding characters, events, relationships, and a storyline of my own invention to create a piece of historical fiction in which *The Scarlet Letter* plays a recurring role.

As of this writing, there are over 8,000 new and used copies of *The Scarlet Letter* for sale on the internet bookselling site ABE

(Advanced Book Exchange) alone and, in the last 160 years, Hawthorne's most well-known book has been read by millions. I recall once seeing a late 19th century copy of *The Scarlet Letter* whose owner, a Miss Ada Carlisle, had inscribed the following succinct comment under her name: "Finished Nov. 1, 1898 – Well worth the perusal." Indeed.

Could Nathaniel Hawthorne have imagined that, so many decades and generations later, his tale of a woman all-at-once a model of courage and the object of public shame would touch so many lives? Unlikely since, when *The Scarlet Letter* was first published in 1850, he predicted that the story would "weary very many and disgust some," his words oddly lacking in both the conventional pride of authorship and the expected writer's recommendation of his work to potential readers. For me, it is the book's subtitle that better provides an insight into Hawthorne's personal view of the story to come: *The Scarlet Letter – A Romance*, those two words revealing that, underlying all the tragic elements, human failings, and broken lives, Hawthorne saw (and sensitively crafted) a story about the power of love . . . a tale that, whether idealistically or perversely, he quite deliberately labeled a *romance*.

Part One: Isobel

"Happiness in this world, when it comes, comes incidentally. Make it the object of pursuit, and it leads us a wild-goose chase, and is never attained."

~Nathaniel Hawthorne

ONE: "THERE IS NO FRIGATE LIKE A BOOK TO TAKE US LANDS AWAY."
-EMILY DICKINSON

I carried the easel stand through the Library foyer and out the front doors, opened the easel's legs and put the announcement in place. The delicate scale of the easel, draped in a black, was dwarfed by the towering stone columns flanking the doorway. Overhead, a bust of Minerva, the Roman goddess of wisdom (and war) looked down on the simple message: *Closed for the Funeral of Miss Isobel Verity.*

"Miss Isobel," as she was known to Norfolk locals, would never again pass through those doors as she had done so regularly since the Library opened a decade earlier in 1904. She was endlessly proud that Norfolk was home to the first free public library in Virginia, an institution made possible in no small part by the generosity of industrialist Andrew Carnegie. Mr. Carnegie, an immigrant from Scotland who writ large the classic American dream of rags to riches, blazed a path from 13-year-old "bobbin boy" changing spools of thread in a Pennsylvania cotton mill to become a magnate of the American steel industry. Also a zealous philanthropist, Carnegie shared his enormous financial success in

1

equally grand fashion intent on giving away the vast majority of his wealth for the betterment of people and institutions. Key to that mission was his certainty that cultivating minds, rather than simply increasing wages, was the solution for raising standards of living. Believing that education was the key to ensuring opportunities for future generations, Carnegie converted that philosophy into endowments for the construction of public libraries in America and internationally.

I should mention that before the Carnegie-funded library was built in Norfolk, there had been local libraries open to the public for some thirty years including the Norfolk Library Association, formed in 1870. Access to those libraries, however, required a paid membership or subscription, something that left many citizens unable to partake of the joys of reading and learning about the world (past and present) through books. Miss Isobel loved literature and, like Andrew Carnegie, believed that literacy was essential to the development of American society at all levels.

I had heard the story (more than once) of the day that notification arrived informing the officials of the city that Norfolk had been chosen to receive a grant of $50,000 for the construction of a permanent free public library. The newly-appointed Library Board members, flush with victory and awash in congratulatory wishes from the leading citizens of Norfolk, convened a meeting to begin making immediate plans for launching the library construction project. As the story goes, Miss Isobel arrived, uncharacteristically, some ten minutes after the appointed meeting start time carrying a splint market basket draped over her arm. The basket appeared full to brimming with an array of fresh produce including carrots, turnips, and beets peeking out from brown paper wrapping.

Board member C.C. Gatling, a gentleman acquainted with Miss Isobel since their mutual childhood years and still fond of "pulling her pigtails" to amuse himself, commented on her having kept her colleagues waiting as she perused root vegetables. His self-satisfied smile was met without a word as Miss Isobel instead placed the basket on the table and removed the wrapped vegetables to reveal a fine bottle of Port and eight crystal glasses each neatly swaddled in a crisp white linen napkin. Ever the gentile southern lady and not to be seen escorting a bottle of wine through the streets of Norfolk, Miss Isobel had cleverly cloaked her cargo in farm-fresh produce. Reportedly, as the flush washed over Mr. Gatling's full cheeks, he reached for the bottle and called for a celebratory toast.

It was three years from the time the Carnegie funding was awarded until the library building was completed. The building site on West Freemason Street was generously donated by the Selden family and the Boston architectural firm of Herbert D. Hale and Henry G. Morse was retained to design the building. The result was a graceful classical structure worthy of its mission as home to volumes that would inform, intrigue, inspire, and spark the imagination of its patrons. For the many who never before had access to a library and the opportunity to borrow books, passing through the front door of the new Norfolk Library must have been a bit intimidating and quite an adventure. I know it was both for me.

Yes, I am a Norfolk girl, born to a farmer's daughter and a local tradesman in 1894. My parents married for love and looked forward to filling their modest home with the chattering and energy of many children. Sadly, I was their only surviving child. Three others were lost in the early months of Mother's pregnancies and my baby brother Luke barely made it into this world only to pass away just weeks later. Mother was emotionally crippled by those losses and I believe she held herself to blame for denying Father more children. She died when I was eight. Well-intentioned friends and neighbors thought to console Father and me by saying that Mother's death was the inevitable outcome of a "broken heart." No one need tell us about Mother's daily struggle with the memories that relentlessly haunted her mind or the singular sadness that took root in her soul. I do not mean to say that Mother did not love me . . . or Father. She pressed on through years of such suffering, caring for us, keeping house and home despite her demons. She said so little about her feelings that, sometimes, Father and I almost believed she was coming out of her very personal darkness. *Almost.*

After her death Father and I, accustomed to our partnership, a reciprocal support system that developed in response to Mother's condition, continued in that fashion making the adjustments to the cadence of daily life necessitated by Mother's absence. We mourned her loss while imagining her in heaven with Luke and the lost babies. At least that is what I did because I could then visualize Mother with her gentle smile and the lightly flushed cheeks so rarely seen in the last years of her life. The lines that had mapped the strain she was under were gone from her face. I hoped that Father could also call her to mind and see her that way, at peace. He was so good to me, so strong for my sake. Should I ever marry and have children of my own, I pray that I will have his balance of strength and tenderness.

Construction of the new library was just beginning at the time that Mother passed away in 1902. Curious, I would often stroll down Freemason Street and linger, watching the workmen. Perhaps because I was an only child or perhaps just because it was my nature, I had (and still do have) a rather fertile imagination. Daydreams were often "excursions" of a sort for me. As I learned to read (something my parents both encouraged), Father would sometimes surprise me with the gift of a new book. Although his business was successful enough to meet our basic needs and a bit more, I knew those book purchases were something of a small luxury for our family and I was duly and sincerely grateful for them.

Among them was Mrs. Prentiss's *Little Susy's Six Birthdays*, a collection of short stories prettily bound in bright green cloth boards with lovely gilt trim. As the title clearly states, the book recounts the events of a little girl's first through sixth birthdays. I took my time reading each of the stories so as to ensure that I felt the passage of each year as Mrs. Prentiss had pointed out that it took three-hundred-sixty-four days following one of Susy's birthdays before it was time to celebrate the next. Susy and her little brothers and cousins were like friends who let me share in her birthday joy and adventures. Susy's visits to her dear grandmother gave me a window into an experience I had not been fortunate enough to have as my own grandparents had left this world before I arrived in it. And then there was the baby house, built for Susy's fifth birthday by her "Papa" and furnished by her "Mama." Even now, I can still readily visualize the illustration of that baby house, a grand two-story and four-room affair.

The book that left the most indelible impression, however, was the one Father gave me just after Mother died. So many years later, I wish I had asked him how he selected it. Of course, the timing of when he gave it to me alone made it memorable. The book was *Little Pussy Willow* written by Mrs. Harriet Beecher Stowe, better known for her both celebrated and decried 1852 book opposing slavery: *Uncle Tom's Cabin*. *Little Pussy Willow*, published nearly two decades later, was written for children . . . for young ladies to be precise. Fairies and spirits bestow their mystical gifts on a baby girl. One of those gifts is "always seeing the bright side of everything," a view of life that makes her the soul of kindness, a child and then young lady who yearns for nothing but to be of service to others. Through the character of Pussy Willow, Mrs. Stowe delivers an important lesson in life values simply expressed by the following line: ". . . it is quite plain that it is not so much what people *have* that makes them happy, as what they think and feel about what they have." A sentiment worth remembering that has served me well. But that was not all I took away from that book. Like me, Pussy Willow, from a family sustained by honorable hard work, had but a few well-loved books to call her own. Among them was Longfellow's epic poem *Evangeline*.

As the new library building sprouted up from the ground I imagined going through the front doors with Father, greeted by rows and rows of shelves holding hundreds and hundreds of books I might read. Where would I start? With *Evangeline*, of course!

On November 21, 1904 the new Norfolk Public Library opened and ushered in the first opportunity for Virginia residents to borrow library books without any cost. A proud community lauded the efforts of the Library Board and the opening of a stately new building in town. Father, having patiently listened to my almost daily updates on construction progress, woke me early and asked if I *might* want to accompany him to the Library so that he could apply for membership. His membership (and later my own) fed and gave haven to my imaginings and became a portal that took me to places and connected me to people and events that changed my understanding of life and of the world, near and far, measured in both distance and time.

TWO: "THE LOVE OF LEARNING, THE SEQUESTERED NOOKS, AND ALL THE SWEET SERENITY OF BOOKS." -HENRY WADSWORTH LONGFELLOW

I happily passed many an hour at the Library over the ensuing years. After a day of school, I would drift in and do my take-home lessons at one of the sturdy wood tables. Looking back, I believe I viewed my "spot" in the corner of the Library with the same sense of possessiveness as the elderly ladies at church services who would, God's house notwithstanding, give the evil eye to anyone who dared sit in "their pew."

In late 1906, both the board and the staff of the Library were preparing (with understandable community pride) for the upcoming Jamestown Exposition of 1907, an enormous fair celebrating the 300th anniversary of the arrival of the famous Captain John Smith and three ships of English colonists who established the first permanent English settlement in North America. While much is said about New England's Pilgrims who landed at Plymouth Rock in 1620, Virginia's Jamestown settlement well-preceded that event. The Exposition was scheduled to open in April 1907 and was expected to attract millions of visitors to the Hampton Roads area during its six-month run. The Norfolk Ladies Club worked tirelessly, creating decorations, banners, and exhibits promoting the Exposition. I envied their involvement and dearly wanted to have a hand in the preparations myself.

One afternoon as the ladies were busily working on their projects, I approached and asked if I could be of any help. Mrs. Watts, the club treasurer, looked up. Just before my interruption she had put down her pen, slowly uncoiling the fingers that had been gripping it as if suffering from cramps. She asked if I had a legible handwriting with neatly formed letters. I politely offered to let her see a sample so she might judge for herself. She handed me the pen and a scrap of paper and I wrote "Jamestown Exposition" as carefully and neatly as I could. She nodded approvingly and with that I began making the first of dozens of labels and cards that would be used on exhibits in the Library and at the Exposition as well.

The Exposition opened as planned on April 26, 1907 despite construction delays and other problems that would bring criticism to those responsible for the management of the fair. Father and I were there on opening day and saw President Theodore Roosevelt who officially opened the Exposition. I especially enjoyed the replicas of the three ships that landed in Jamestown in 1607: the Godspeed, the Susan Constant, and the Discovery, and marveled at the nearly life-size recreation of Philadelphia's Independence Hall. Father and I returned to the Exposition at least three more times before it closed and discovered something new with each visit. I read later that over three million people came to the fair, some "experts" and newspapers characterizing that number of attendees as a "disappointment" and pronouncing the Exposition a financial "debacle." I should mention that I did see some of my carefully written labels attached to exhibits in the Virginia building at the fair, something that delighted both Father and me.

My work on the labels was apparently mentioned to the Library Board as I received a lovely thank you note on their behalf signed by Miss Isobel as board secretary. I do not recall exactly when I first noticed Miss Isobel and the fact that she, like me, was a regular habitué of the Library. Sometimes she oversaw book circulation activity at the helm of the imposing oak desk that greeted visitors to the Library. I observed that she had a gift for remembering people's names and I duly noted the effect that talent had on the patrons. She was one of those people who could disarm with a smile and smoothly do two things at once – chatting and engaging people while deftly completing a borrowing slip at the same time.

A woman in her maturity, perhaps fifty or so years old, she had the air of a much younger person – not in a foolish way but as if somehow her soul or spirit had remained youthful while her physical person had aged. I found myself watching her at times and confess that, at home, I sometimes imitated her way of speaking and mannerisms in front of the small wall mirror in my room – surely an example of the proverb "imitation is the sincerest form of flattery." While a gentile and well-bred lady, Miss Isobel was no retiring violet. Never married, a "spinster" to some, she had developed a sense of confidence, a presence that traveled with her, and opinions freely and frequently expressed whether asked for or not. I wondered how in heaven's name I might imitate those attributes in front of my mirror!

Among Miss Isobel's opinions was that the Library should initiate programs to promote patronage by both adults *and* children. The conventional wisdom was that the very presence of the Library and the resources it offered was quite enough to warrant the citizenry's interest and participation. As for children, the responsibility for encouraging reading vested in their parents and teachers. Miss Isobel acknowledged the logic of that argument – as it related to the more financially well-off in the greater Norfolk community. Her objective was to cast a much wider net and reach the children of the population whose work days began with the rising sun, wound down only as the sun gave way to the evening shadows, and often extended across all seven days of the week. Andrew Carnegie would have applauded such an idea.

In June 1908, an announcement was published in the *Norfolk Beacon* inviting parents to register their children for the new twice-weekly reading program that offered storytelling and other group activities for youngsters between the ages of six and nine. The ad also said that individuals interested in volunteering to assist with the program should contact Miss Isobel Verity at the Library. I was sure I was the right person to be one of the reading program volunteers since I was so acquainted with the workings of the

Library. Also, being a volunteer would mean working more closely with Miss Isobel, an added benefit and exciting prospect in my eyes. I stood in front of my faithful bedroom mirror, chin lifted for effect, and practiced how I would offer my assistance to Miss Isobel. Surely a mature young woman of fourteen with my knowledge of the Library would be an asset to the children's program.

I needn't have fretted. The candidate pool was a small one – myself and the Widow Boone were the only ones who expressed an interest. Mrs. Boone, having lost both her husband and only child to cholera, relocated to Norfolk to be near her only living relative, a bachelor brother for whom she kept house. The role of wife and mother tragically stripped away from her, she turned to nurturing her new community by acts of volunteerism, no doubt hoping to once again feel a sense of purpose to her life. She was both kind and generous in her efforts but, while grateful for her contributions, people mostly kept their distance due to a fear of having to broach the subject of the deaths of her husband and child. If she noticed their reticence, she did not show it or seem aggrieved by it. I understood their fear all too well having seen the awkwardness that came between my mother and even her closest friends after my brother Luke's death. I wondered if Mother and Mrs. Boone might have become friends if they had met. Could their mutual pain have brought understanding and consolation? Perhaps such a friendship would only have intensified their burdens and drove them to a deeper hell on earth. There was some serendipity in the way that Mrs. Boone was put into my path for, if anyone could reason her out, I believed I could. As Mother had been, Mrs. Boone was a damaged vessel slowly leaking its lifeblood. One day, fully drained of that spirit, she would simply fade away from this earth and reawaken in heaven wrapped in the arms of her husband and child. Until then, we would be busy bringing the joys of reading to the children of Norfolk.

Registration was slow at first with less than a dozen children having been signed up by their parents. Miss Isobel responded to that with the sweetest of incentives, designed to appeal not to the parents but directly to the children themselves. When the youngsters arrived for the first week's classes, she brightly welcomed them, praising them for their good sense in being among the first to secure a place in the program. She spoke with wide eyes and much gesticulation describing some of the stories and characters they would "meet" over the coming weeks. Then she masterfully solidified their attention by casually saying that their good sense should be rewarded and would be. Every one of them would be getting a licorice stick to take home when class ended.

The story of the tasty licorice stick reward echoed through the schoolyards of the lucky recipients and had the desired effect: enrollment nearly tripled in short order and, yes, Miss Isobel made sure to give each new attendee the same reward at the conclusion of their first session. She also let the children know that those who came to classes regularly during the six-week program would receive a certificate of merit at the last session. They say you never get a second chance to make a good first impression. Amen!

Things were going very well with the reading program as the weeks went by and we prepared to offer a second six-week program to follow the first hoping that word of mouth (favorable of course) would bring us more children for the second series of sessions. Miss Isobel asked me to meet her at her home to look through some new books she had ordered for the program so an outline could be created for the upcoming sessions. I had never been to her home, a fine row house off Granby Street, and I was both excited and a bit nervous about going. I rang the bell and a ruddy-faced, middle-aged woman with ginger hair and wearing a crisp white apron opened the door. I gave my name and she ushered me in saying she would let Miss Isobel know I had arrived. I would soon learn that her name was Katie and that she was from Ireland and had been in service as Miss Isobel's housekeeper and cook for many years.

Miss Isobel walked me into the parlor and I saw what must be the new children's books neatly stacked on one of the matching demi-lune tables that flanked the fireplace. Taking in the whole room, however, it was what was hanging above the fireplace that captured my attention. Momentarily lost in looking at the portrait that hung there, I heard Miss Isobel's voice and turned toward her not sure what she had said to me.

She asked if I found the portrait "interesting" and I replied that the subject, a young woman with wavy chestnut brown hair and a warm tawny tone to her skin, was beautiful and a bit "exotic." She politely stifled a laugh and before she could say more, Katie came in with a steeping pot of tea and biscuits. Miss Isobel thanked Katie and then, gesturing to the painting, told Katie that I was taken with the "exotic" subject. That provoked a wide grin from the Irish woman who, taking pity on my being at a loss to understand what was so amusing, informed me that the exotic creature was Miss Isobel. In an instant, Katie's ruddy cheeks were no match for the shade of red that had come over my own.

Katie gave me a wink and left the parlor. I tried not to look at the portrait (or at Miss Isobel) with no success. I glanced over at Miss Isobel's upswept finely coiffed white hair and her delicately-lined ivory skin and then at the portrait. The awkward silence was broken when she wryly commented that while her portrait was unchanged from the day the last brush stroke touched canvas, its subject had clearly "faded" over the years. I don't remember exactly what I said next but when I attempted to apologize for my reaction to the portrait and the revelation that she was the sitter, she waved her hand dismissively which I took as a sign that it was time to get to work on the reading program outline that had brought me to her home. Not so.

Miss Isobel poured for the two of us and we enjoyed the oven-fresh biscuits. Returning her delicate bone china cup to its saucer, she looked directly at me and confessed that her true purpose in meeting with me was not as she had told me. Her request was related to the reading program all right but nothing so simple and innocuous as picking out story books for the next sessions.

As she had hoped, interest in the reading program was growing by word-of-mouth and as a result of local schools being on summer recess which meant more free time and more need to occupy homebound youngsters. Among the newest crop of registrations were several for Negro children, news that delighted Miss Isobel but was received with trepidation and a mild air of panic by the other members of the Library Board. At the board meeting earlier that day, there was considerable animated back and forth about how to handle the situation. Miss Isobel held her own but knew that if it came to a simple majority vote, she might not prevail. She paused for a moment to tell me that she did not believe that any opposition to registering the Negro children was rooted in the board members' personal racial prejudice and pointed out that while some of the board members were more "progressive" than others, all of them, excepting herself and C.C. Gatling, had been born after or in the waning days of the War of the Rebellion and grew up after the time when Americans dressed in blue and gray had raised arms against each other.

Miss Isobel refilled our tea cups and only when I lifted the cup to my lips did I realize that my jaw was clenched, no doubt in sympathy with the knot that had formed in my stomach. In my personal delight at having a free public library available to *me*, I had never once considered that its doors were not open to every resident of Norfolk, a realization that would alter my awareness and affect my way of thinking from then on.

After a sip of her tea and another nibble on her biscuit Miss Isobel continued recounting the events at the board meeting. Mr. Gatling, knowing nothing useful would come from the ongoing cacophony, suddenly rose from his chair and admonished the board members to "keep their heads" and put their considerable mental prowess to work finding common ground and compromise. *Compromise.* That one word cut through the fog of voices and viewpoints and an idea was born. The Negro children would have their own reading program, to be held in the small annex building behind the Library. Borrowing from the "separate but equal" premise that governed segregated public education for "colored" children, the board members could hardly be subject to any criticism for their decision. Miss Isobel, well-schooled in picking her battles, suppressed her objection to the program being relegated to the annex building. Instead, she elicited a promise that she would be the one who had the last word as to the *equality* of the program for the Negro children. With that proviso agreed to, the matter was settled and as the old saying goes: what was sauce for the goose would also be sauce for the gander.

THREE: "EDUCATION IS NOT THE FILLING OF A PAIL BUT THE LIGHTING OF A FIRE."
-WILLIAM BUTLER YEATS

We set to work preparing for the new reading program, Miss Isobel's personal interpretation of equality guiding the way. While using the books from the original children's reading program, she also created some additional class materials as well. She wrote several short stories, including one about Mr. Frederick Douglass who was quoted as having said: "Once you learn to read, you will be forever free." I brought in my own treasured copy of *Little Pussy Willow* knowing full well that Miss Isobel would approve as the book would naturally provide an opportunity to tell the children a bit about Mrs. Harriet Beecher Stowe who had departed this world not many years before.

The day for the first Negro reading class arrived with a respectable registration of eight children. I was setting out the materials when Mrs. Boone appeared. I say *appeared* rather than *arrived* with deliberateness. She had this way of entering the room without a sound sometimes giving me a start when I turned to find her right behind or beside me. Miss Isobel joined us soon after and casually remarked (for Mrs. Boone's benefit) that today's session would be the start of a new reading program . . . for Negro youngsters. For a fleeting few moments Mrs. Boone, caught utterly by surprise, looked askance at Miss Isobel and her mouth worked as if she would speak. That reaction was gone in seconds, however, replaced by the slow blossoming of a satisfied smile and a rare glint of light in her small dark eyes. The new reading program, complete with licorice sticks, certificates of merit and, at Miss Isobel's personal expense, a book for each child to take home as their own, produced wide eyes and much rapt attention among the children and was by all measures in our opinion a very successful undertaking.

The end of the summer months brought the return to school for the children of Norfolk, including me. I was to start classes at the high school where I would be part of a much larger body of students than in my local primary school, an exciting but also intimidating prospect. One evening as Father and I ate our supper meal and I was going on as usual telling him the latest about Miss Isobel, Mrs. Boone, and the goings-on at the Library, he interrupted wanting to talk about my upcoming start of classes at the high school.

Father was a tinsmith. His many years of experience and his attention to detail were evident in his work. He could do something as routine as repairing a handle on a favorite old stew pot, giving it many more years on the stove top. He did a lot of such repair work for families and for local restaurant and hotel kitchens. I always enjoyed watching him work no matter what the project but seeing him at work on a new piece, whether commissioned by a customer or for his own inventory, was something quite apart. In his hands a lifeless sheet of tin was transformed, becoming a thing of graceful curves, pleasing proportions <u>and</u> utility: a candlestick, snuff box, lantern, or perhaps a locking document box with arched lid. His talents and reputation notwithstanding, however, there was no doubt that the recent industrialized manufacture of household and decorative items was bringing readily available stock at lower prices to local store shelves, presenting a challenge for tradesmen like Father.

That evening, Father had good news to share. He had been very busy in the last several weeks with both repair work and two new commissions and, always thinking of me, had put aside a small amount for me to buy a new dress for my first day of high school. My immediate instinct was to refuse his kindness as it seemed unwise to spend the money that way. Then I remembered *Little Pussy Willow*, the book he gave me when Mother died. That purchase was made at the same time Father had to pay for Mother's final medical and burial expenses, a time when resources must have been seriously stretched. That book was more than a gift for a grieving child, it represented a bond between Father and me. I stood up from the table and went to him delivering a hug and kisses much like I did that day so long ago when *Little Pussy Willow* entered my life. The dress was selected: a lovely pale blue fabric with a pattern of petite white flower buds, cuffs and collar trimmed with a narrow band of lace. Miss Isobel and Mrs. Boone agreed that I had made a very fine choice. The look on Father's face when I left for my first day of high school left no need for me to ask what he thought.

The autumn months that year were cooler than usual and as the Christmas holidays approached, Virginia got the season's first snowstorm. Under the headline "Virginia Wrapped in Snow Blanket," the *Richmond Times Dispatch* reported on conditions across the state. A "blinding snowstorm" brought nine inches to Winchester and eight inches to Front Royal. In Staunton and Charlottesville, well over a foot of snow accompanied by high winds deposited drifts four feet high. In the eastern portions of the state there was less snow but the storm, a severe northeaster, lashed Norfolk and other coastal towns with alternating rain and snow and winds reaching forty miles an hour.

On Christmas Eve morning, Father ventured outside to check for damage to the roof of his workshop building that sat next to our house. As the wind was wailing the night before, we heard the corrugated metal roof groaning and feared the gale might actually lift or rip it from the building sending it sailing through the air like a rusty magic carpet. The rain and sleet were still coming down hard when Father went out to inspect the damage and he was thoroughly drenched when he came back to the house. The roof was still in place but would need repairs, the immediate problem being the continuing risk of water damage to his equipment and supplies in the workshop. Father insisted on going back out to wipe those down and then cover them with tarps to prevent any further water damage. I reached for my coat and boots intending to go with him but he would not allow it. When he finally came back in I met him with towels and a dry set of clothes. After he had changed, I wrapped him in a quilt and brought him a hot cup of tea with a small shot of whiskey. I fretted. He assured me he was "fine." In the end, he would not be "fine" and all my fretting could not change that.

Father ate poorly on Christmas Day and I would not let him go to church services. I hoped he was simply drained from his exertions of the prior day but by that evening he began to cough. In the night the cough grew stronger and more frequent and fever came on. I sat with him most of the night applying plasters and wiping the sweat from his brow. Dr. Heath came to us the following day and pronounced Father down with an ague. Over the next few days, despite my and Dr. Heath's best efforts, Father's condition worsened. The fever would not break and the fits of coughing shook his whole body.

Hearing about Father's illness when she stopped in at the Library, Miss Isobel came to our house and, clearly alarmed at Father's state, arranged for him to be transported to the Sarah Leigh Hospital in Ghent. It would be to no avail. Despite the fine and modern care the hospital offered, Father passed away three days later and my world was forever altered. Under a biting wind that thrust the tears from my cheeks, his mortal remains were laid to rest with Mother and Luke on January 2nd, the first Saturday of the new year, 1909. I did not worry about the cold hard earth that would surround him. I knew in my heart that his soul had already flown to the heavens and he was happily reunited with Mother and Luke. Someday, I would join them and our family would be whole again.

Miss Isobel graciously invited me to stay with her for a while but I declined as I needed to be at home to collect myself and accept that Father was really and truly gone. I had stayed at Father's bedside during his three days at Sarah Leigh and was then kept occupied with the plans for his burial leaving me no time to think about the prospect of living alone . . . of being alone . . . of *our* home becoming simply *my* home. There was nothing to be gained by putting off that reality. Delaying it would surely make it even more of a dreadful reckoning. I was nearing my 15th birthday and was not a "child" as were some young people of that age. Father said I was "born old" but I remembered the days when I would pray to the Almighty that I might grow up faster and stronger so I could do more for Mother, helping her and Father both with their burdens. Anyway, it mattered not what my reasoning was. I must now be ready to be responsible for myself.

Among the kind notes of condolence I received was one from Mr. C.C. Gatling, Miss Isobel's friend. I recalled Mr. Gatling having work done by Father on a few occasions but couldn't imagine that prompting a personal note. I read the last sentence of the note twice to ensure I was understanding the words: "Kindly come to my office on Granby Street at your earliest convenience and do bring Miss Isobel as I must talk with you about your father's estate." I was at first perplexed, that confusion followed by concern. Perhaps Father had unpaid bills or had taken a mortgage on our house to shore up our finances. It was one thing to adjust to living alone in our home but quite something else to find out that it must be sold to satisfy outstanding debts. The loss of the house would break my last earthly connection to my parents and give my definition of "alone" a devastating new aspect.

As soon as I could pull myself together, I went to see Miss Isobel, Mr. Gatling's note in hand. Miss Isobel was already aware of the summons from Mr. Gatling. I steadied myself and explained that I feared Father had left debts or a mortgage and that the meeting would bring bad news. She took my face reassuringly in her dainty hands as she called for Katie to bring her coat, scarf, and hat. As soon as those had been put on, we were out the door and on our way to see Mr. Gatling.

As I listened to Mr. Gatling, the look on my face changed from a mask of concern to one of disbelief. There was no mortgage nor were there unpaid debts. Unbeknownst to me, Father had apparently been putting aside small sums of money for quite some time, depositing those funds at the Merchants and Planters Bank on Liberty Street. One day several months ago as Father was leaving the bank, he met Miss Isobel who was coming in. Father nervously asked Miss Isobel not to mention to me that she had seen him at the bank. Miss Isobel, well-intentioned, asked if something was wrong. Father then confided that he had opened an account at the bank for my benefit and did not want me to know. His plan was to turn the account over to me on my eighteenth birthday to use as I saw fit – perhaps to enroll in a local college.

As he requested, Miss Isobel kept his secret from me but she entrusted it to someone else: Mr. Gatling. C.C. Gatling was a member of the board of directors of the Merchants and Planters Bank. His father had been an accountant and the younger Gatling had his father's gift for numbers. At the age of seventeen C.C., with his father's encouragement and dressed in his Sunday best, walked into a local Norfolk bank and asked for the branch manager. He boldly asked for a job, offering to show the manager his aptitude for figures. The manager, aware that young Gatling's father was a very competent accountant, offered C.C. a two-week unpaid trial position. From that humble beginning grew a long and successful career as a senior banker and financial advisor.

Mr. Gatling had been advising Miss Isobel for decades. His investing approach was predicated on growth _and_ asset preservation. Miss Isobel said he dubbed his method "collar and cuffs," comparing a sound investment plan with a well-tailored shirt: it must uniquely fit its owner. Miss Isobel laughed as she told me that she had once heard another of Mr. Gatling's clients refer to the method as "collared and cuffed," suggesting an image of C.C. Gatling as a Pinkerton in hot pursuit of fugitive stocks and bonds. When Miss Isobel told Mr. Gatling about Father's desire to create a nest-egg for my future, he offered to provide investment advice if Father was agreeable. Father gratefully accepted his generous proposal.

Mr. Gatling explained the various small investments that had been made with the account deposits and offered to continue providing his advice if I wanted to proceed in that way. He suggested selling Father's equipment and trade supplies, possibly at auction, to add to the account funds and said a monthly disbursement would be made to me for my living expenses. Going forward, he would review the portfolio with me at least quarterly to ensure that I was informed as to my financial situation and to permit me the opportunity to make changes if I desired. There was one more thing. Father had asked Miss Isobel to be my legal guardian should he die before my eighteenth birthday. Utterly speechless as I listened to Mr. Gatling's words, I had forgotten she was sitting in the chair beside me. I slowly turned to her. She put her hand over mine and squeezed gently. I wanted to say something but the words would not come. My mind was full of thoughts of Father . . . his unselfish love . . . his sacrifices for my future . . . and his wisdom in putting me in Miss Isobel's hands.

Miss Isobel and I agreed that I would remain living at home for the time being as that was what I particularly wanted. I returned to school in mid-January and I took on a part-time position at the Library that paid a small stipend and helped with pocket money. As the term ended and summer recess began, Miss Isobel invited me to go to Ocean View for lunch at a favorite place near the pier, an invitation I happily accepted. Ocean View was a much-frequented resort attraction drawing both locals and tourists seeking respite or recreation that could be enjoyed in the form of a stroll in the sun, a lounge on a sandy beach, a spin on a ride in the amusement park or a wager put down at its casino.

It was a lovely Saturday in late May, warm and sunny. We took the streetcar from downtown to Ocean View at about eleven o'clock. The crowds were a good deal thinner than they would be a month later when summer excursions to the beach and amusement park would draw thousands of visitors. A little too early for lunch, we took a leisurely stroll and then sat on a bench enjoying the breeze off the bay as we watched people passing by.

Over a delicious lunch of fresh local seafood, we talked about goings-on at the Library including the sad news that Mrs. Boone's brother had died after a fall down a steep flight of stairs. I wondered why a merciful God would visit repeated tragedy on such a gentle woman. Eventually the conversation turned to the next school term. I had assumed I would continue at the high school for at least two more years. Miss Isobel had another idea. She explained that, at my age, she had been very fortunate to have been sent to a female academy in New Jersey. Her mother, not a wealthy woman but "comfortable" was, like philanthropist Andrew Carnegie, a disciple promoting the value of education . . . for all children.

Miss Isobel said she had talked with Mr. Gatling to ascertain whether funds were adequate to consider my attendance at such an academy without jeopardizing my overall financial security. He reviewed the current state of my portfolio and projections for the next one to two years and gave Miss Isobel a figure that could be prudently spent on tuition. She had already looked into a number of schools and had whittled the list down to three that met with her approval.

As my eyes passed down the short list, the first thing I noticed was that not one of the three schools was in Virginia. My stomach, comfortably full with a fine seafood lunch up to then, began to flutter and an awkward silence filled the air. Finally, stating the obvious, I pointed that out. Miss Isobel, having left home and her dear mother when she attended school in New Jersey, read my reaction without any need for elaboration on my part. She told me how she had sobbed on the train ride from Richmond to New Jersey. Neither the new dresses in her lovely tapestry valise nor her new Spanish leather boots and matching gloves had any effect on her misery. When her sobbing was spent, she pouted in silence. So went the trip up North.

She was met at the rail station in Trenton by the assistant headmistress accompanied by a fair-haired teenage girl with bright blue eyes, no doubt a student at the school. Miss Isobel was civil and respectful to older woman, nothing more. She did better with the young woman who sat next to her and offered to be her student body "partner," providing every possible assistance during her adjustment to life at the Saint Mary's Hall Episcopal School. Later that evening as she settled in her room and prepared for the formal orientation activities in the morning, the corners of her mouth turned upward for the first time in days. She was thinking how clever it was of the assistant headmistress to bring a student with her when she came to the train station, diffusing potential tension with the presence of the blond-haired girl (whose name was Lucy).

The first few weeks at the new school were punctuated with bouts of homesickness but that waned as Miss Isobel became absorbed in an array of studies and activities that whet her academic appetite and naturally created a feeling of belonging. Saint Mary's Hall was established in 1837 by Right Reverend George Washington Doane, second Bishop of New Jersey, who purchased a small Quaker academy near the Delaware River. Recognizing that young girls were a largely ignored and grossly underserved group when it came to education and seeing the folly in that, Bishop Doane determined to do differently. Renaming the former academy Saint Mary's Hall, it became a boarding school with the mission of offering education to girls from grades seven to twelve, enabling them to live "whole, intelligent, complete Christian lives."

Looking back upon graduating from Saint Mary's, Miss Isobel was thankful for her mother's wisdom and resolve in sending her away to school, an experience that enriched her fertile mind and rewarded her with friendships lasting to this day. She smiled as she reminisced, recalling the day she said a special private good-bye and thank you to Lucy, the girl who had greeted her at the rail station two years earlier when she had made her "saucy" descent from the train in Trenton. Lucy's offer of assistance and the friendship that grew from it were remembered even now with gratitude. All these years later, Miss Isobel deftly recited a remembered stanza of a poem written by Bishop Doane entitled "Written on Leaving Home:"

> *I leave thee, dearest, for a while,*
> *Yet leave thee with our God;*
> *His sheltering wing is o'er us still,*
> *At home and when abroad.*

I understood the opportunity I was being given and embraced it, setting off to school in Maryland, a destination far enough removed to seed my independence yet comfortably positioned border to border with my dear Virginia, thus feeling not that distant from home. Before I left, Mrs. Boone, bless her, offered to visit my house weekly to dust, open windows, and the like, ensuring that all was in order during my absences. I countered with another scheme; I asked if she would actually occupy the house while I was away. I had heard that the house she had lived in with her now deceased brother was not owned by him but was under a lease. I knew it was too large (and likely too expensive) for her and having her live in my house seemed a perfect arrangement for both of us. As I expected, she demurred and began to give excuses for not accepting my offer. I was careful not to appear or sound as if my offer had any aspect of charity or, worse yet, pity. She slowly came around to my plan . . . on her terms. She would pay a modest rent for occupying the house, reasoning that *both* of us would benefit from that arrangement. Miss Isobel congratulated me on having had such a fine idea and for my equally fine "negotiation skills."

My almost three years at the Maryland boarding school were much as Miss Isobel had described her time at Saint Mary's. The breadth of areas of study far eclipsed anything that the Norfolk public high school system could have offered. That is not to say that I would not have received a good education had I stayed in Norfolk. In a way, it is like food. You can be healthy and sated consuming simple nutritious meals comprised of staples like meat, potatoes, fruits, and vegetables but it is something quite different to be able to partake of a banquet table of food options, tastes, and textures. So, for the time that the banquet table was open to me, I did not hesitate to fill my plate with a variety of study topics and experiences that enlightened and intrigued my mind or challenged my way of thinking.

There was for me, however, another kind of awakening that recalled me to a conversation I had with Father not long before his passing. That discussion happened about the same time Father had surprised me with the gift of a new dress to wear on my first day of high school. He mentioned that I would meet many new young people in high school and said he was sure I would make many new friends. Friends? I couldn't recall us ever before talking about that subject. It was true that I had not developed any close relationships with children my own age that I knew from school or church. I must admit I had never really given that any thought and, more telling, was the fact that I had no recollection of ever feeling lonely for such companionship. What I did feel then was guilt for causing Father even a moment's concern by my seeming detachment from people my own age. Father needn't have worried. The adolescent girl who left Norfolk for boarding school returned quite altered in that regard. Immersion in a colony of budding young women, most away from home and family for the first time, was fertile ground for bonding. Books and study tips were not the only things exchanged among the female student body. Whispers, giggles, secrets, and dreams were freely shared with trusted confidants along with contraband copies of fashion magazines and romance novels that were definitely not on the approved reading list. I recall Miss Isobel's narrowed eyes and mildly pursed lips when I returned home for the Christmas holidays with rouge on my cheeks. The things we learn in school!

My time at boarding school ended on brisk spring day in 1912 when I had just turned eighteen. Miss Isobel, Mrs. Boone, and Katie all attended the diploma ceremony and the reception and dinner that followed. My emotions spilled over in tears when I saw that all three of them had come and, the following day when I said my good-byes to my teachers and the friends who had become so integral in my life, hankies were once again needed. We promised to write to each other and to visit as well and I had every certainty that my eyes would meet theirs again one day.

The train ride back to Norfolk was lively with me chattering on about the final days at school as my companions patiently listened. I described the signing of autograph albums with clever ditties, the arrival of family members (and sweethearts), and a number of special events for the graduates including a surprise visit from Mrs. Edith Houghton Hooker, the cousin of one of the graduating girls. Seeing no sign of recognition on their three faces, it was going to be my great pleasure to tell them all about Mrs. Hooker.

I turned to angle myself in my seat so I could see Mrs. Boone and Katie across the aisle. (Miss Isobel was sitting next to me.) I began to excitedly (and apparently a bit too loudly) talk about the amazing Mrs. Hooker, a leading Maryland suffragette. Katie and Mrs. Boone looked around nervously and showed me their best forced smiles. Miss Isobel tried to keep a straight face as she remarked that it would probably be best to keep our conversation "a bit more private" as some of the other passengers might be "napping or absorbed in their newspaper." From nearby, I suddenly heard the rustling of pages, no doubt meant to reinforce Miss Isobel's surmise. I regrouped and went on.

A year-and-a-half earlier, Edith Houghton Hooker, a graduate of Bryn Mawr College and one of the first few women admitted to the Johns Hopkins University School of Medicine, formed the Just Government League, an organization advocating giving women the right to vote. The wife of a doctor, she had become a social worker in Baltimore where she also established a home for unwed mothers.

At the invitation of her cousin, Mrs. Hooker came to our school several days before graduation . . . arriving in her own automobile! She praised the school and our teachers for their commitment to educating the young women who would not only be wives and mothers but also community leaders and voters who would bring the considerable common sense and decency of the female gender to bear on our country and the world. She boldly challenged us to use our energies and knowledge for the betterment of working class women and children and in the eradication of poverty and illiteracy. For several moments immediately after she concluded speaking there was not a sound in the hall but then, suddenly, the room erupted in applause.

Katie let out an involuntary "whoop" when I finished as if she had been in the hall with me that day. Mrs. Boone looked dumbstruck, mouth agape. Miss Isobel, smooth as ever, said she would be at the front of the line to register to vote as soon as the politicians "got out of the way." But I wasn't finished yet. I took a deep breath and served up the finale: Mrs. Hooker had taken five of us for a ride in her automobile which was festooned with banners proclaiming "Votes for Women," telling us we were the first official attendees of her new automobile tour meetings. I think I squealed out loud at that point and collapsed back in my seat, now ready for *my* nap. Mrs. Boone leaned across the aisle no doubt thinking Miss Isobel was in need of comforting and, as I dozed off, I thought I saw Katie cross herself in the way that Roman Catholics do.

FOUR: "IF YOU HAVE A GARDEN AND A LIBRARY, YOU HAVE EVERYTHING YOU NEED."
-CICERO

Mrs. Boone had kept up my little house with such dedication, her efforts returning to me something quite better than the domicile I had left in her custody. Beyond generally treating my modest family home with great care and respect, she had clearly made recent extra efforts in anticipation of my post-graduation return as I observed improvements even since my last visit during the Christmas holidays. The old stove had never been more spotlessly clean and the smells of soap and polish mingled with the fragrance from a vase of flowers adorning the small dining table. All dust had been banished, even that which would normally have taken covert residence in my book stacks. Delicate lace curtains adorned the parlor windows as well as the single window in my bedroom. Simply made with perfectly straight seams and hems, I knew immediately that they were the work of Mrs. Boone's own deft hands.

Those kind hands had been busy outside the house as well. The little front porch was dressed with four terracotta pots of flowers that, with their rainbow of colors, said "welcome" to those approaching the front door. Not ignoring the rear of the house, Mrs. Boone had cleared a patch for a vegetable garden where infant sprouts were already reaching for the sunshine. How to adequately thank her, a woman of such a humble nature that she wilted under the slightest ray of praise?

Rather than any attempt at an overt "thank you for this and thank you for that," I devised a different plan. Over a casual cup of tea the day after we arrived home from Maryland, I put down my cup and slowly rotated my head, taking in a view of the entire parlor. Pursing my lips just a bit and with a slight sigh, I said that I wondered how I would be able to keep up the house and garden as I must seek employment as soon as possible. I continued by saying that the house and grounds were so far improved from what they had been (even with my own best efforts in the past) and I was loathe to think that might change for the worse. And so, with my trap laid, I looked at her with an expression that was to convey the rapid arrival of a "Eureka!" moment on my part and quickly followed that with a plea that she remain resident in the house with me as a solution to my dilemma.

Mrs. Boone considered for a moment and agreed to stay "on a temporary basis" saying that time would tell if the arrangement was necessary. To be honest, there were at least a few kernels of truth to my ruse. This being the second time I had applied my "cleverness" with the objective of maneuvering Mrs. Boone for what I believed to be her own best interests, it occurred to me that she may have seen through me as if I were as transparent as the window panes now dressed in her lace curtains. Mrs. Boone, although so naturally self-effacing, was a woman with common sense and wisdom sculpted from her life experiences. I hoped that if she had caught on to me, she also reasoned out that I was motivated by the best of intentions and a sincere affection for her.

That settled, it was time to start getting my new life in order. No better way to begin than with a consultation with Miss Isobel. I called in to her home and was met with a hug from Katie. Miss Isobel was in the library and I entered to find her seated behind a lovely old carved mahogany desk on top of which were several neatly organized stacks of paper. She looked up, lifted pen from paper, and greeted me with her usual bright smile. I sat in an armchair in front of her desk and she came around and occupied the matching chair, facing me. We exchanged small talk about the graduation and laughed a bit while reliving my antics in telling the story of my encounter with the suffragist Mrs. Hooker. Miss Isobel said, with intended exaggeration, that I all but "scandalized" Mrs. Boone and had set Katie into a "papist frenzy." I made to apologize for my lack of decorum on the train but Miss Isobel cut me off saying that it would be a "fine thing" if all the "indiscretions of the young" should be so inconsequential and so rooted in a "healthy intellectual exuberance."

From the corner of her desktop, Miss Isobel retrieved a small package wrapped in tissue and a red ribbon, handing it over to me. It was a graduation gift from her. I opened the ribbon and peeled back the tissue to reveal a copy of the book *The Scarlet Letter* by Nathaniel Hawthorne, long recognized as New England's finest novelist. The book was not new. Its brown cloth covers were worn, the corner ends bent inward toward tanned inner pages. Its spine, like the backbone of an elderly person, had lost much of its youthful strength and in consequence the book had an aspect of looseness and curvature rather than being tight and square. In the jargon of booksellers, the volume was "shaken." I opened the book to find an inscription bearing the former owner's name, "F. A. Bentell, New Orleans."

I was acquainted with Hawthorne's story of a woman named Hester Prynne who, in mid-17th century Puritan Massachusetts, was condemned to wear a crimson letter "A" upon her chest to identify her as an adulteress to all who encountered her. That badge of immorality and the scorn that resulted from it were the means by which she was to be punished for bearing a child out of wedlock and refusing to name the man who fathered the illegitimate babe. Unlike the typical convicted felon sent off to prison, Hester Prynne's sentence, to be served out in public, had no stated term, its duration subject to the opinions of local leaders and the community that relentlessly judged her day after day. While the book was included in a recommended reading list given to us at boarding school, the subject matter (based on my above understanding of it) signaled a serious undertaking and I had heard wind of the fact that there would be no happy ending for Hester Prynne. Thusly persuaded that *The Scarlet Letter* was not for me, I had turned my reading time instead to something two centuries more contemporary, the autobiography of women's suffrage pioneer Elizabeth Cady Stanton: *Eighty Years & More: Reminiscences 1815–1897.*

While the pages of the copy of The *Scarlet Letter* I held in my hands had a story to tell, I was sure this book (and Miss Isobel) had another still for me to hear . . . and I was right. The gift of this particular book had a duality of purpose and significance intended by the giver. Miss Isobel began by talking about Nathaniel Hawthorne and the novel she described as his "most brilliant work." Hawthorne was born in the first decade of the nineteenth century in the town of Salem, Massachusetts, a place made infamous in the last decade of the seventeenth century for an episode of mass religious hysteria that spawned accusations of witchcraft and culminated in the executions of twenty citizens convicted of that "crime," nineteen by hanging and one "pressed to death."

Hawthorne, a descendant of the very Massachusetts Puritan race at the center of those witch trials and executions, including one of the trial judges, found that ancestral legacy anathema to himself. The incongruence between his Puritan forbearers' flight from their English homeland in search of religious tolerance in the American colonies and the absoluteness and inflexibility of the code by which they governed their own community affected him deeply and so played a significant role in the settings and themes of his literary works.

Hawthorne's father, a sea captain, died when Hawthorne was a boy of not yet five years old leaving his mother, siblings, and him to be supported by the generous assistance of extended family members who would eventually finance Hawthorne's college education. Hawthorne began writing with the hope of publication after his college graduation and had some minimal success but, in about 1840, left Salem to take a short-lived position with the Custom House in Boston, an experience that would later be resurrected to set the scene that introduces the story of Hester Prynne as told in *The Scarlet Letter*. Literary success did come later in the decade of the 1840s leading up to the publication of *The Scarlet Letter* in 1850. Its wide appeal and critical praise took Hawthorne somewhat by surprise it seems, he having predicted that it would "weary very many and disgust some" and describing it as a "hell-fired story."

Miss Isobel, recommending most strenuously that I read the book at my "earliest opportunity," commenced talking about the story in the context of its "eloquent" manner of capturing the essence of a woman all-at-once a model of courage and the object of public shame; a woman so far superior to the men closest to her, their characters degraded and their lives poisoned and broken, one by vengeance and the other by hypocrisy and cowardice. In reading the book, she suggested that I keep sight of the fact that this very fine portrait of a woman was crafted by the very fine mind of a man, something that, to her mind, elevated its message and value all the more.

Lest that enthusiastic endorsement fall on deaf ears, she had one more thing to recommend the reading of *The Scarlet Letter*: my interest in women's rights as evidenced by my support of the quest for women's suffrage. In reading *The Scarlet Letter*, said she, I would better understand the courage and strength that is native to the female gender and that remains the glue that bonds together the fabric of society at all levels, rich or poor, noteworthy or unnoticed. She made her point with examples spanning the ages, calling up the likes of Joan of Arc, Clara Barton, Harriet Tubman and Mary, the mother of Jesus Christ. I took her point, indeed I did.

At that juncture, Miss Isobel took a much needed breath during which Katie came in with a tray of tea and small sandwiches. She cocked her head in my direction and lifted her eyebrows playfully. I had no doubt that she had been eavesdropping from the nearby hall and, with perfect timing, staged her entrance to deliver the much appreciated refreshments. To be honest, I often happily lost track of the hours when spending time with Miss Isobel as her storytelling prowess was second to none in my world. Whether expressing a dearly-held opinion or recounting some recent event or decades-old memory, I was invariably drawn in as the tale was unwrapped and fell in alongside her for the journey.

I swallowed my last bite of sandwich and asked what I had wanted to know since I first opened the book: who was F.A. Bentell? That question was answered with an unusually brief response: F.A. Bentell was Frederick A. Bentell, originally of Norfolk, later of Louisiana, and a now-deceased relation of Miss Isobel through her mother. I waited for more. Instead, Miss Isobel casually mentioned that I had said I had an appointment with C.C. Gatling that afternoon. Recalled to reality, my head turned abruptly toward the tall case clock in the corner and in seconds, a quick good-bye said, I was up and out of the chair and on my way to my meeting with Mr. Gatling.

Entering Mr. Gatling's office I saw an unfamiliar face, a well-built fair-haired young man I took for a few years older than me and likely a new junior clerk or bookkeeper in Mr. Gatling's employ. He looked up as I closed the door behind me and then stood. I walked toward him, gave him my name, and said I had an appointment with Mr. Gatling. Before he could announce me, Mr. Gatling came into the outer office and greeted me, ruddy-cheeked and sporting his trademark cigar.

We sat at a work table in his private office and he began to provide me with a detailed status of my investments. I admit to having had some concerns about what he would tell me as there had been an economic recession over the past year and there were many people whose financial situations had experienced serious setbacks. Those who had heavily gambled their financial security on a predicted continued rise in stock prices and investment yields suffered terrible losses. I remembered Miss Isobel's story about Mr. Gatling's personalized "collar and cuffs" investment methodology. Hopefully the news would not be bad.

My portfolio results for the last two quarters were only slightly down (beyond the amounts used to pay my school and living expenses), some investments having held steady or made a modest gain, others having losses that were not severe. If I had not appreciated or shown much interest in the concept of "asset preservation" previously, I was now a disciple ready to proclaim its good news.

Mr. Gatling and I discussed my finances in light of a possible desire to attend college. I admitted that, at present, I was unsure about continuing my education, even if financially feasible, as I was undecided as to what course of study I would pursue . . . and to what professional end. While I had been inspired by the knowledge of some of my teachers and could not deny the mark they made on young minds like my own, their sphere seemed insular to me and their participation in the world at large somewhat vicarious through the students they schooled and sent out to spread their own wings. I mentioned how I had admired Father for being "his own man" of business, albeit a modest enterprise. While no captain of industry, he only answered to himself (and to the shifting sands of customer tastes and economic cycles) in his decision-making and, of course, bore the weight of the wisdom, success, or failure of those decisions. Mr. Gatling, ever the pragmatist and always a source of sagacity, complimented me for my thoughtful assessment of my future saying that I had an insightfulness beyond my years that would serve me well. In the end, we arrived at a plan whereby I would seek employment, work for a year, and then revisit the decision to go to college or not. He reminded me that there were fine institutions offering two-year advanced education programs, something I could consider as a form of compromise should I still have uncertainty at that time.

After finishing the discussion of my financial position and educational dilemma, Mr. Gatling called out to the new clerk whose name was Andrew Pritchard asking him to bring in the accounting of my expenses for the last quarter. Young Mr. Pritchard had apparently been charged with putting that accounting together. He brought the paperwork in and turned to leave the office but Mr. Gatling called him back instructing him to go over the expenses with me. Mr. Pritchard and I went through the accounting line by line, my final boarding school tuition payment representing the greatest portion of the total paid out. Everything in order and understood, I thanked him for his time, bid him and Mr. Gatling goodbye, and headed into the street in the direction of my next stop, the dry goods store, to retrieve Mrs. Boone's order of thread and fabric for a new tablecloth she planned to make. I confess that, lost in thought, I walked right past the door of the dry goods shop. Those thoughts, centered on Andrew Pritchard, kept me company for the rest of the day and only left me as the haze of sleep took me away that night.

The next morning I chastised myself for my schoolgirl preoccupation with Andrew Pritchard and blanched at the thought of how I would have excitedly described meeting him to my boarding school sisters were I still in residence there. Moreover, I awoke to see Miss Isobel's gifted copy of *The Scarlet Letter* sitting unopened on my bedside table reminding me what I should have been doing as I lay in bed the night before. That day and the following one were consumed with errands, working on a list of my skills and capabilities to aid in my search for a new position, visiting the cemetery to put flowers on my parents' grave . . . and thinking about Andrew Pritchard.

Before graduation, we were required to attend a two-hour training session on the elements of creating a curriculum vitae to provide to potential employers or college admissions personnel. The instructor claimed that he had seen a facsimile of a form of resume letter crafted four hundred years ago by none other than master artist and inventor Leonardo Da Vinci who was seeking employment with the powerful Duke of Milan. Imagine that.

I spent more than an hour at the cemetery. It was a beautiful sunny day with an almost cloudless soft blue sky. There is a bench near my parents' grave. Sometimes I linger there talking softly to Mother and Father. Other times I just sit silently in the quiet. Either way, the feeling of peace there refreshes me. Both evenings, I set aside a bit of time before retiring to read a few pages of *The Scarlet Letter*.

The next day I was to meet Miss Isobel at her request. I was anxious to tell her that I had started reading the book and to find out more about its former owner, Frederick A. Bentell. On my way, temptation got the best of me and, on a newly-minted pretext, I stopped in at Mr. Gatling's office hoping Andrew Pritchard might be there. He was. As before, he stood when I entered and approached him. My heart beating fast, I told Andrew that I had need of a copy of the accounting of my last quarter expenses that he had recently gone through with me as I planned to discuss it with my guardian, Miss Isobel Verity. I asked if he would please make a copy of those ledger pages that I could pick up the Monday following, thus allowing him three days to write it out. He said he would "certainly" do so and would have the accounting ready for me on Monday morning. With that, I thanked him and made my exit, somewhat astonished and ashamed at my behavior and the casualness with which I concocted and acted out such a blatant falsehood. As I walked down the street past the long row of windows showcasing goods for purchase at Smith & Welton, I deliberately kept my gaze focused straight ahead to avoid catching my reflection in the glass lest I see the crimson flush that was no doubt rising on my burning cheeks.

I spent that afternoon with Miss Isobel as planned. I told her that I had started reading *The Scarlet Letter* and was surprised at the humorous and somewhat irreverent tone of the introduction to the story that described the goings-on at the author's former workplace, the Boston Custom House. Remembering her telling me about Hawthorne's repudiation of his ancestors' role in the horror of the Salem witch trials, I mentioned how he had made that clear in the introduction to the book calling two of those men "bitter persecutors" and declaring the bones of one of them stained with the blood of the women martyred as witches. Miss Isobel smiled and said that the book's introduction had raised the ire of many Salem locals and, Hawthorne being Hawthorne, he soon added a preface to the next edition recognizing the public furor and, tongue squarely in cheek, rejected accusations calling his description of the climate and frequenters of the Custom House "malevolent." For his part, he commented that he could not have written it "in a better or kindlier spirit" or "with a livelier effect of truth." He concluded the new preface by saying he would not change a word of the introduction.

I told Miss Isobel what had been discussed at my meeting with Mr. Gatling and about my plan to work for at least a year before deciding about attending college. She agreed there was no hurry and said working for a while would help with the cost of college should I decide to go. I showed her the curriculum vitae I had crafted for my job search and she replied that she knew of a position I might look into. The Norfolk Library had received a generous bequest from the estate of Mr. H. D. Van Wyck, the benefactor stipulating that it be used to establish a second library location in the greater Norfolk area, a small "branch" to serve the needs of those living a distance from the main library on Freemason Street. The head librarian, Mr. William H. Sargeant, had authorized the hiring of two new library staff to provide administrative support for the branch planning process. She casually asked (as if she needed to!) if that might interest me. I made quick work of getting my capabilities list over to Mr. Sargeant, hoping that my attachment to the Library as a volunteer and part-time employee would help my cause. I knew I could ask Miss Isobel to recommend me to Mr. Sargeant but I did not ask as I so wanted to get the position based on my own education and history of involvement at the Library. I was scheduled for an interview the following week with the assistant head librarian who told me that Mr. Sargeant had reviewed my capabilities and added me to the final list of candidates for consideration.

On Sunday after Mrs. Boone and I returned from church services and were about to sit down for our mid-day meal, there was a knock at the front door. Mrs. Boone motioned to me to stay at the table and she went to answer the door. I heard a male voice talking with her and, in a few moments, she came into the room accompanied by Andrew Pritchard. He had introduced himself to Mrs. Boone as a clerk working for Mr. Gatling and said he had an "accounting report" that I had requested. Andrew smiled and handed me an envelope containing the copy of the expense ledger. He said he remembered that I needed it for a "meeting" and thought to bring it by so that I would have it in case that meeting was first thing the following morning. His consideration, based at least in part on my original lie, threatened to bring the hot flush back to my cheeks.

Before I could thank him, Mrs. Boone asked if he had yet eaten lunch. He hesitated for a moment before answering and Mrs. Boone, interpreting that as a response in the negative and a reluctance to impose, told him to join us. I say "told" him because, uncharacteristically, her tone was such as to leave him no choice.

The meal went well considering my surprise at Andrew's appearance and his at being asked to stay to eat.

I awoke the next morning thinking it might have been a dream and was delighted to recall it was not. Hope, accompanied by the devil known as "pride," joined together to convince me that Andrew's kindness was prompted by his personal interest in me and desire to make a good impression. I thanked Mrs. Boone for inviting Andrew to stay to eat. When she smiled in response, I saw her brows rise, giving her the distinct appearance of a co-conspirator.

My happy mood came with me later that week when I had my interview for the position at the Library. I thought I did well but did not know how many others were under consideration for the two openings. It was a long two weeks until I heard the good news that I had been selected for one of the administrative positions. If Miss Isobel spoke to Mr. Sargeant on my behalf, I do not know. I hoped she had not.

FIVE: "YOU EDUCATE A MAN, YOU EDUCATE A MAN. YOU EDUCATE A WOMAN, YOU EDUCATE A GENERATION."
-BRIGHAM YOUNG

I finally got the opportunity to ask about Frederick Bentell. It was more than worth the wait. Mr. Bentell was a first cousin to Miss Isobel's mother Emmeline. Emmeline's father, Benjamin Ricardo, and Frederick's mother, Sarah Ricardo, were siblings. Both the Ricardo and Bentell families had ties to Norfolk stretching back about a hundred years, to the early 19th century. Frederick's father, Henry Gustav Bentell, was originally from Pennsylvania and came to Virginia during the War of 1812 as a sergeant in the United States Marine Corps stationed at the Gosport Navy Yard near Norfolk. He served on the 38-gun frigate *USS Constellation*, launched in 1797 as the very first ship commissioned by the United States Navy. In 1813, a small fleet of British frigates, schooners, and cutters sailed into Hampton Roads signaling an imminent attack on the Norfolk area. At the Gosport Navy Yard, the *Constellation* was anchored along with some two dozen armed sloops and schooners, Sergeant Henry Bentell being one of only a few officers on board. The British ships mustered in the bay and soon began sending hundreds of redcoats off toward shore in barges. Approaching the shore, many of the barges became bogged down in the mud, falling victim to rounds fired from the *Constellation* and the other American gunboats from Gosport. That and other stories of Henry Bentell's laudable service in the Marines during the War of 1812 were proudly passed down in the family, children like Miss Isobel hearing the tales from their parents or at family gatherings.

After his service in the military, Henry Bentell remained in Norfolk where he met Sarah Ricardo, born in Charleston, South Carolina. Sarah had come to Norfolk not long after Henry's arrival at Gosport, her intention being to open a school for young ladies. The school offered instruction in needlework and drawing, music lessons on instruments such as the piano forte, and academic classwork in reading, writing, and arithmetic. Sarah's school enterprise ended sooner than expected when she married Henry Bentell in 1816 and the newlyweds began a family, their first child being Frederick Bentell. After leaving the military, Henry began a new career as an agent for Norfolk's *American Beacon* newspaper. He served in that role for some twenty years, a fixture at the publication's news and reading rooms and a well-known newspaperman in Norfolk.

At the time of Henry's death in the early 1840s, he was engaged in a business dispute that arose from a change of ownership of the *Beacon*. When he fell ill, he told his wife Sarah that the newspaper owed him a large amount of money representing unpaid wages and commissions. He said that he had been offered $300.00 to settle the debt but refused to accept that amount thinking it an unfair discount of the sum actually owed to him. When he died his son Frederick, then about twenty-five years old, was appointed to handle his father's affairs and found the family's financial situation strained. Frederick, concerned about the security of his mother and youngest siblings, did what he could to stabilize the situation. Upon hearing about the debt owed by the Beacon, he wrote to the former owner under whose management the unpaid wages and commissions had accrued, asking to reopen discussions about the disputed amount with that man and the new owner. Putting his pride aside in that letter, Frederick admitted that receipt of the owed amounts was crucial to the security of his mother and the futures of his younger siblings who desired to finish their educations. An agreement was reached and a payment was made to Frederick on behalf of his widowed mother. In addition, impressed with Frederick's maturity and concern for his family responsibilities, the newspaper owners arranged for Frederick to meet with a contact of theirs involved in hiring for government agencies. Through that referral, Frederick was offered a position with the United States Postal Service . . . in New Orleans. The opportunity was too good to pass by. Just a year after his father's death Frederick, then newly-married, relocated to New Orleans taking his wife Mary Jane, mother Sarah, and youngest siblings with him.

Miss Isobel's mother Emmeline was a favorite of her aunt, Sarah Bentell, and Emmeline was also a close friend of Frederick Bentell's wife Mary Jane, the two women having been schoolgirls together in Norfolk. Emmeline was born a "late in life" only child to her parents and had spent considerable time in the company of her Bentell aunt and cousins. Their removal to New Orleans was a most considerable loss for her and, then nineteen years old, she entertained thoughts of going with them but knew she could not. Her parents' health was already in a fragile state and she was very much needed in Norfolk. Her father Benjamin had achieved some success as a local merchant and Emmeline had helped by working in his shop, keeping it going until her father's health would no longer allow. Unlike Henry Bentell, Benjamin Ricardo was prudent and organized in the management of his business and personal finances. When he passed away, Emmeline and her ailing mother were left reasonably secure, their home being without a mortgage encumbrance and there being funds in the bank along with some investments sufficient to guarantee them a comfortable existence for years to come. Emmeline's mother, as is often the case with the loss of a spouse, seemed to lose her desire for life and, despite Emmeline's considerable efforts to fill the void left by her father's death, quickly followed him to the grave.

After her parents' passing, Emmeline closed up their home, retaining a caretaker to see to its maintenance and protection, and made arrangements for ship passage to New Orleans. She spent nearly four happy years with her Aunt Sarah and her cousin

Frederick's family who were delighted to have her with them once again, Frederick's wife Mary Jane being particularly glad to have her "sister" returned to her. In similar fashion to her Aunt Sarah who, relocating from Charleston to Norfolk decades earlier, had opened a small teaching establishment for girls, Emmeline became a tutor working with young girls to improve their academic skills in specific areas of weakness or struggle. Her advertisements in the *New Orleans Crescent* were met with rather more interest than expected and it was not long before her services were much in demand.

The move to New Orleans had brought new prosperity for the Bentells as well. Frederick was a respected route agent for the Postal Service and was talked about as a likely candidate for the position of Deputy Postmaster. True to his words in the letter he had sent to the owners of the Norfolk *Beacon*, Frederick saw to it that his siblings were educated, including his youngest sister who herself became a teacher. In keeping with their father's career in the newspaper business, Frederick's two younger brothers Henry Jr. and Virgil were employed at the *Crescent*, each of them with aspirations of becoming a reporter for that publication.

Occasionally during Emmeline's time with her Bentell relations, visitors from that clan made their way to New Orleans. The Bentell line originated in Germany, prior generations having emigrated from there to Pennsylvania where they replanted roots that spawned new American branches, Frederick's father Henry being one of the fruit to blossom thereon. Henry and his wife

Sarah had remained close with the Bentell branch in Philadelphia and it was those relations who would come to spend time in New Orleans, often to escape the harsh winter season at home. Emmeline found them charming company and they embraced her as if one of their own. During their periodic stays in New Orleans, evenings were spent in lively conversations sharing news from each of the families along with more serious discussions about the state of politics and other timely topics. Sarah proudly recounted how well her children were doing and how successful Emmeline's tutoring service had become and the Philadelphia visitors did likewise as to their branch of the family. There was no aspect of competition in these exchanges. Each side was a supporter and promoter of the other and claimed as their own any success on either front. That is most clearly illustrated by the role the Philadelphia Bentells played in Emmeline securing a most fine teaching position in New Jersey.

Weeks after they had departed New Orleans to return to Philadelphia, Emmeline's Aunt Sarah received a letter from them. Upon reading it, she showed the letter to Emmeline without comment, waiting to see Emmeline's reaction to the contents. As Sarah waited she struggled with immediate conflicting feelings of excitement and dread, neither of which she intended to show Emmeline. Emmeline, like her aunt, was conflicted and looked at Sarah trying unsuccessfully to divine her thoughts. The letter contained an offer of a position at the Saint Mary's Hall academy for girls in Burlington, New Jersey, just across the Delaware River from Philadelphia. The Bentells, acquainted with the founder of that school, Bishop George Washington Doane, had inquired as to openings on the teaching staff. Being told that with the expanding student body there would be two to three new teachers being taken on for the next term, they gave their ardent recommendation that Emmeline Ricardo be considered for one of the openings. They penned a form of reference letter enumerating Emmeline's qualifications, emphasizing her work in multiple subject areas with students who were not thriving in school. The Bishop, much impressed with that breadth of experience, agreed that Emmeline seemed a very good fit for the school. The letter, explaining the foregoing, asked that Emmeline send word "immediately" of her willingness to travel to Philadelphia for an interview with the Bishop and his headmistress.

The decision was an agonizing one for Emmeline. The thought of leaving her dear family was unsettling yet the opportunity to continue her teaching career at such a level in such a well-respected institution was more than tempting. Her Aunt Sarah firmly refrained from giving advice or counsel, fearing to influence Emmeline one way or the other. Her cousin Frederick was not so reticent. Having taken the risk of relocating his family to New Orleans in response to a promising job offer, he encouraged her to do likewise. He reminded her that while she could always return to them and New Orleans, she would not likely get another chance like the one being offered to her. She could not deny the common sense logic of his argument. Knots in her stomach notwithstanding, Emmeline responded to the letter saying that she would be most pleased to come up for the interview.

Before her departure, she and Frederick's wife, her dear Mary Jane, spent a day shopping for two new dresses, a bonnet and a more sophisticated hat, matching gloves, and a new pair of shoes. Emmeline was unaccustomed to such splurges but enjoyed sharing the hours and decisions with Mary Jane, who only asked in return that Emmeline promise to write regularly and come back to them during school adjournments. Emmeline reminded Mary Jane that her employment was subject to the outcome of the interview with the Bishop and headmistress and she might be back sooner than anyone thought.

She did not come back, for several years in fact. As expected, she was hired for a teaching position at Saint Mary's Hall and quickly became a favorite of both the school administration and her students, so much so that she was asked to stay over during the summer breaks to offer remedial classes to students who were struggling academically. Initially limited to just a few classes, the summer program ultimately expanded to also offer the greater student body a session of classes that would accelerate their graduation from the academy. Emmeline not only taught select summer classes, but also served as headmistress of the summer sessions. Her deep involvement in the school became her "life" and left little time for her to return to New Orleans or Norfolk. On the infrequent occasions when she did take a well-deserved day or two of rest, she most often spent that time with the Bentells who generously opened their Philadelphia home to her and encouraged her to visit with them as often as possible.

Emmeline's caretaker in Norfolk suggested that she rent out her former home and, with her agreement, oversaw the process of finding reputable and respectable tenants and collected rents on her behalf. She wrote faithfully to Mary Jane, Frederick, and her Aunt Sarah and they did the same in return. She was missed in New Orleans but things were going well there as Frederick was appointed Deputy Postmaster and his brothers had become reporters at the *Crescent*. Only Mary Jane's letters spoke of the sadness that she and Frederick were still childless.

Emmeline's return to New Orleans would be precipitated by a confluence of unanticipated events. During the last summer session she oversaw, several of her students were stricken with cholera during an outbreak of that disease in the greater Philadelphia area, one of the girls dying despite all efforts to save her. Emmeline feared greatly for the other three girls and suspended classes in the hope of reducing the spread of the disease. She visited the hospital in Philadelphia daily and spent the rest of her time caring for the sister of one of the cholera victims. The sisters were from Mississippi and had lost their mother at a young age making them very much attached to each other. Amanda, the sister who had contracted the cholera, was just one year older than her sister Henrietta, whom the students called "Hattie." Hattie was nothing short of terrified at the thought that her sister might die. So far from the home where they lived with an aunt, uncle, and their three brothers, Hattie was well and truly "alone" for the first time. Emmeline insisted that Hattie stay with her in her small apartment at the school rather than in the dormitory. She saw to it that Hattie ate meals despite her saying she was not hungry and watched the young girl for signs of the onset of the dreaded cholera. Thankfully, Hattie did not contract the cholera and her sister Amanda rallied and began to recover as did the two other girls from the school. When Amanda was well enough, she and Hattie made the trip home to Mississippi and, showing the uncanny resilience of youth, left assuring Emmeline that they would return to finish their education at Saint Mary's when all was right again with Amanda. Emmeline wrote to their aunt and uncle to fully explain what had transpired and weeks later received a note from them confirming that the two girls had reached Mississippi safely and remained of a mind to return to Saint Mary's in the future. Good as their word, the sisters later did return to Saint Mary's but, by then, Emmeline had returned to New Orleans. Hattie became a regular correspondent with Emmeline and the connection made in those dark days of Amanda's illness was the foundation for a life-long friendship.

Emmeline's decision to leave Saint Mary's was not the direct result of the cholera outbreak. The winds of social unrest and the festering political conflict between the northern and southern states were becoming more troubling and Emmeline found that she sometimes felt isolated from her fellow teachers and the school administration and reluctant to enter into conversations about those tensions. Still, even that might not have been enough to make her go back to New Orleans but when she received a letter from Frederick saying that Mary Jane was not well, the decision was easily and quickly made.

Upon arriving in New Orleans, Emmeline was met by Frederick at the wharf. He was often there in his capacity as route agent and Deputy Postmaster checking on and directing the flow of incoming and outgoing shipments of mail traveling by ship. The news about Mary Jane was good in that she seemed to be regaining her strength but the cause and effect of her "illness" proved devastating. Mary Jane had been pregnant, news that made her and Frederick deliriously happy after so many years of trying to have a child. She forbid Frederick to tell anyone in the early months as she was apprehensive due to having had a miscarriage some years before. Frederick was sure his mother Sarah suspected, however, as Mary Jane often looked tired and sometimes fled the table saying she suddenly felt ill or was not hungry, all signs of early stage pregnancy. Midway through her fourth month, she and Frederick made plans to tell the family their good news but it was not to happen. While Frederick was at work one day, Mary Jane was seized of sudden cramping that escalated into sharp pain that put her in bed. Before Mary Jane asked, Sarah sent for the doctor believing the pregnancy was in jeopardy. There was nothing that could be done as nature in its seemingly arbitrary perversity was acting to take another unborn child from Mary Jane's womb. Mary Jane hemorrhaged terribly and, for some hours, Frederick and his mother thought she would also be taken from them. She survived, weak of body and broken in spirit, her mind in torment over the loss of her baby. More than that, the miscarriage and bleeding had left no possibility that she could ever carry another child.

When Emmeline arrived at the house with Frederick, Mary Jane was resting in the parlor, her small stocking feet perched on a tapestry covered stool. She managed a smile for Emmeline who came across the room, knelt next to the chair, and covered Mary Jane's pale face with kisses. Emmeline's gift for helping those who were struggling, such as her students, would be redirected with all its power to Mary Jane's struggle to regain her physical strength and surmount the tragedy that had changed her life and dreams for the future. People sometimes say that "time heals all wounds" but that is not true so for many . . . including Mary Jane Bentell. She would not find a true reason to live until the turmoil of a war and an occupation of New Orleans by Union military forces that came some years later.

SIX: "MOTHER IS THE NAME FOR GOD IN THE LIPS
AND HEARTS OF LITTLE CHILDREN."
-WILLIAM MAKEPEACE THACKERY

I had been watching Miss Isobel's many facial expressions as she told me about her Bentell family. Her eyelids slowly closed at some points as if she felt their emotions or was sharing in their experiences. She seemed almost transported back in time as she talked, once again with her mother who undoubtedly told her these stories many years ago. After speaking about the sorrow that befell Mary Jane Bentell she paused, her head moving almost imperceptibly in a side-to-side movement that spoke of compassion for Mary Jane. I used that opening to ask if she would like to wait until another time to continue the story as it was then approaching five o'clock. She agreed it was a good idea to stop at that point, there being quite a lot more to the story. I said I would come back on Sunday afternoon if that was convenient for her. She said it was.

As I walked home, I tried to review and take in all Miss Isobel had told me about the Bentells and her mother Emmeline. For one thing, I now knew why Miss Isobel had been sent to school at Saint

Mary's Hall in New Jersey: her mother had been a teacher there. Although Miss Isobel had talked at great length and with considerable detail about the Bentells, her mother's closeness to them, and the trials that had befallen her mother's aunt and cousins, she had mentioned nothing about when and where her parents had met and married. I realized that I could not think of an instance when she had ever spoken of her father. When she spoke about her childhood in Norfolk, which was not often, she made references to her mother and sometimes to Mr. Gatling, but never really mentioned anyone else. I knew that, even as an adult, she had remained living with her mother Emmeline until that lady passed away about twenty-five years earlier. Could her devotion to her mother have been the reason that she had never married . . . assuming she *had never* married? Once again my curiosity was off and running.

On my way to Miss Isobel's house on Sunday afternoon, I stopped by the bakery to pick up some of their wonderful blackberry scones. As I hoped, a fresh batch was just coming out of the oven and the box was still warm when I rang the bell at Miss Isobel's. Katie, Miss Isobel, and I devoured the scones which were served with clotted cream for good measure and capped it off with a pot of Miss Isobel's special Assam blend tea. Stomachs quite full, Miss Isobel prepared to continue telling me the story of her Bentell relations.

Despite Miss Isobel's mother Emmeline's sincerest efforts to comfort Mary Jane Bentell on the loss of her unborn child and notwithstanding Frederick's patient, loving attentions to his grieving wife, she remained listless, inconsolable, and lost in her thoughts. Frederick, so genuinely concerned about his wife's condition, had no time to mourn his own loss. His mother Sarah did whatever she could to support him . . . and Mary Jane. From time to time, there were small breaks in the clouds of sorrow that hung over Mary Jane and very slowly she found her way to some level of "acceptance" over the months that followed. Frederick kept busy with his activities as a Mason and became a much-respected officer of the local New Orleans chapter. Soon, however, they would hear the drums of a civil war that would bring another significant disruption to life as they knew it.

In November 1860, Abraham Lincoln was elected President of these United States and before he could be inaugurated the following March, southern states had begun to secede and rejoin together as the Confederate States of America, under President Jefferson Davis. In April 1861, just a month after Lincoln took office, the first shots of the War of the Rebellion (known in the North as the War Between the States) were fired at Fort Sumter, South Carolina. One year later, the city of New Orleans fell to Union naval forces and was under occupation and martial law for the duration of the war.

The occupation years (and the ensuing years of the Reconstruction) were ones of suffering and humiliation for the citizens of New Orleans who, as suspected or acknowledged Confederate supporters, lived under the oppressive regime of the appointed Union Military Governor of New Orleans. The once bustling Port of New Orleans, at first crippled by a Union blockade, was reopened as a major distribution center for Union military support thus attracting an influx of Northerners looking to take advantage of the opportunity to reap the profits of that activity, legal and illegal, both methods condoned by Union authorities who filled their own pockets in the process.

Had they known what was coming, Emmeline, her aunt, and cousins might have accepted the generous offer from their Philadelphia relations to come to them and take refuge in Pennsylvania until hostilities ended. Frederick Bentell, a Deputy Postmaster at the time New Orleans fell, had worked under Postmaster Riddell, a Northerner appointed to his post by former President James Buchanan. Riddell, opposed to secession, welcomed the arriving Union naval officers at the Customs House and escorted them around the city as they prepared for occupation.

Having taken an oath of loyalty to the Confederacy, Frederick steadfastly refused to throw that off when demand was made of him to do so. He was forced to register as an "enemy of the United States" and subsequent to that, in 1863, was compelled to leave his home and seek refuge behind the Confederate lines where he remained for over a year. When a change in military governor brought a means for him to return home he came back, painfully thin and physically compromised from his ordeal. He submitted to house arrest for the remainder of the war and was subjected to periodic interrogations by Union officers. Frederick's brothers

Henry and Virgil had both enlisted in the Confederate Army but Frederick, lame as the result of a childhood injury and in his forties, was not fit for service.

During the absence of the Bentell men, the women of the family cleaved together. Emmeline, Mary Jane, and Sarah, then in her seventies, knew they were being watched for any sign that they were in communication with Frederick, Henry, or Virgil or were aiding them in some way. The three women employed their time helping other women and children left on their own and also ministered to the sick during a short-lived outbreak of yellow fever in the city.

When Frederick came home, he found a change in the household that had been left to the management of the ladies of the family. Mary Jane had taken in an orphaned child, a girl appearing to be about eight years old at the time he returned. The child had been one of those the women had cared for during his absence. She was a frail frightened child when she came to them and did not speak at all. Thinking her a deaf mute, they kept her with them for a longer period and, during that time, Mary Jane became so attached to the child that she refused to give her up. Frederick found quite a different child when he came home. After a year with Mary Jane, Sarah, and Emmeline, the child's rosy cheeks spoke of good health and only a jagged scar at the hairline marred her pretty face. Although a timid child, she was not deaf as originally believed and under Mary Jane's care had slowly begun to speak once again. Frederick saw clearly that the prosperity of the rescued child had rekindled his wife's dampened spirit, a thing of no small consequence.

Some months after Frederick's safe return, Emmeline determined that she would try to go back to Norfolk to find out the state of her family home and with thoughts of resuming her independent life. She was grateful to have been with her family during the war years and they, especially Frederick, felt indebted to her as well. Booking passage would take several weeks during which time she sent a letter to her old caretaker in the hope that he would have news of her home and conditions in Norfolk.

Beyond her memories of the past and hopes for the future, she had but a few things to take with her to Norfolk. When she opened her tapestry bag to begin packing up her few clothes and possessions, she found something in the bottom of the bag. It was a copy of *The Scarlet Letter* by Nathaniel Hawthorne. Mary Jane, remembering how Emmeline would read aloud from that book in the lonely evenings during Frederick's absence, gave her their copy as a reminder that they would always be with her.

As the date for her departure was nearing, Emmeline received a letter from her Norfolk caretaker who reported that while her home was not badly damaged, it had been occupied by squatters during the early days of the Union Army occupation of the city and would need some repairs before she could return to living in it again. The caretaker provided an estimate of the time and cost to do so and Emmeline wrote back authorizing him to proceed and instructing that he send her progress reports as the work was being done. He also reported that the city had seen some "recovery" from the darkest days of its early occupation when there had been a terrible shortage of food, no work, and a flight of local residents. Emmeline was surprised to see that he had credited the most recent Union military governor, General Benjamin Franklin Butler, with restoring order and improving dire conditions. It was that very man who served as the first military governor of New Orleans and had kept his boot squarely and harshly on the necks of the people of that city.

Emmeline's news that her departure would be postponed was greeted with wide smiles from Frederick, Mary Jane, and Sarah. Perhaps the hand of fate played some role in the rearrangement of Emmeline's plans as more misery was about to be visited upon her beloved Mary Jane. The day after Emmeline explained the situation with her Norfolk house, Mary Jane accompanied her to the ticketing office to cancel her ship booking. It was a beautiful day and they decided to walk back, stopping in at a café for a glass of lemonade on the way home.

Emmeline could tell all day that something was bothering Mary Jane. As they left the café and began walking arm-in-arm as was their custom, Mary Jane dropped her head and began to cry softly. It was then that she told Emmeline that she had found a hard lump in her breast weeks earlier and had sought medical help in secret so as not to alarm Frederick. After two consultations, one with a general physician and a second with a surgeon, she had been told just days before that the diagnosis was cancer . . . and that surgery would need to be performed as soon as possible. Thinking Emmeline would be leaving and not wanting to cause her to change her plans, she had withheld the bad news.

Emmeline kept her composure but was devastated and very frightened for Mary Jane. No surprise to Emmeline, Frederick was even more so when he was told. The surgery was performed and Mary Jane came through it as well as could be expected. Frederick left no stone unturned in seeking treatment and curatives for Mary Jane, including some things that Emmeline doubted had any therapeutic value such as the much-advertised Claremont Spring Water he had purchased. Newspaper ads touted the discovery (one year earlier) of a mineral spring in the Ozark Mountains whose waters had proven curative for a whole array of diseases from cancer to piles. Mary Jane dutifully drank what seemed like gallons of that liquid, she and Frederick convinced it was helping her recovery. The purveyor of the product, ever anxious to have testimonials to its efficacy, even convinced Frederick and Mary Jane to write a glowing report that was then published in their newspaper advertisements. The water delivered no cure nor did it prevent the reoccurrence of Mary Jane's cancer that returned in the form of another lump, this time in the pit of her underarm. She fought death like a warrior, unyielding in her objective to remain with her husband and her adopted child, battling until the very moment that her last breath ended her suffering.

Mary Jane's death came just weeks before the end of the war. Frederick was without a job or prospects and as he and Emmeline sat together after Mary Jane's burial he confided that he had no idea how he would raise a child without her. His mother Sarah was too old and in compromised health herself and could not be expected to become a surrogate mother for the little girl. Emmeline had been thinking the very same things herself but had been reluctant to say anything to Frederick. She had a solution in mind and proposed it to him and Sarah: she would "adopt" the child and take her to Norfolk. The little girl knew her well as Emmeline had helped with her care and even served as a tutor for the child, thus creating a bond between them. Since Mary Jane's illness, she had spent even more time with the child and believed that would make the transition easier for the girl and less traumatic than having Emmeline leave her so soon after the loss of Mary Jane.

Frederick and Sarah saw the merit of Emmeline's argument but were concerned about her reputation. How would she explain her motherhood on her return to Norfolk? The adoption had not been done through legal channels, complicating the situation. Emmeline said she would simply say that she had married in Louisiana and had since been widowed. She proposed to use Mary Jane's maiden name "Verity" as the surname of her deceased husband. She said she was all but certain that the disruptions of the war would provide ample cover and, should anyone ever come forward to challenge her, she would simply tell the truth: that the child was an orphan rescued during the war and was put into her care lest she wander the streets and die of hunger or disease.

The decision made, Emmeline and the child departed for Norfolk just after General Lee's surrender at Appomattox in the spring of 1865. After the defeat of the Confederacy, her cousin Frederick was able to apply for a pardon under a proclamation issued by President Andrew Johnson. His pardon with amnesty for his "offenses" arising from his participation in the "rebellion" was finally approved in consideration of his age, the physical disability that ensured he had not served as an active Confederate combatant, and his taking of the required amnesty oath. His two brothers returned safely from the war although Henry had fallen ill during his service and died several years later. Frederick's mother Sarah died just a few years after Mary Jane and, sadly, Frederick himself passed away in 1875 at the age of fifty-eight. Miss Isobel reached over to retrieve an envelope from a nearby table, removed a yellowed newspaper clipping from the New Orleans *Times-Picayune,* and read from it:

> "We are called upon to mourn the sudden and untimely loss of Frederick A. Bentell, a man of the highest virtues whose character illustrated the tenderest emotions known to the human breast. An upright citizen, a devoted husband and son, affectionate brother and a true friend, he was in all the relations of life a model of unswerving devotion to duty. Mr. Bentell was a native of Norfolk, Virginia, whence he came to this city nearly thirty years prior. He was for many years engaged in the Postal Department of the Government, serving as Deputy Postmaster and Special Post Office Agent, the arduous duties of which responsible positions he discharged with conspicuous

ability. A life-long Mason, he was devoted to the order having been appointed secretary of several such bodies including that of the Grand Lodge, Masons of Louisiana. His proficiency in his duties is attested by the praises it elicited and the degree of veneration in which he was held. His largely attended funeral was presided over by Dr. Palmer who gave an eloquent Christian service, solemn and impressive. Mr. Bentell lived an unostentatious but useful life and has left behind him the sweet fragrance of a character unblemished."

My eyes were as round as the full moon when I realized that the little orphaned girl was Miss Isobel and moist with tears at the tribulations that befell the Bentell family. So engrossed in the unfolding drama of the story, I never noticed that Katie had come in and sat down near us. I suddenly had a feeling of déjà vu. Here I was in Miss Isobel's parlor, speechless once again, just as I had been the day I first saw the "exotic" portrait over the mantle and, as then, my bewilderment was apparently most amusing to Miss Isobel and Katie. When I recovered myself, tea was served and I attempted to pepper Miss Isobel with more questions to no avail. She did promise to one day tell me how her mother Emmeline's cousin Virgil, a well-known maritime reporter for the *New Orleans Crescent*, had been instrumental in forwarding the literary career of author Mark Twain by agreeing to publish the then river pilot's early writings in his column in the *Crescent*. In return I offered the promise she had not asked for, that being my pledge not to reveal, to anyone, the story of how she came to be Isobel Verity.

SEVEN: "WHAT I BEGAN BY READING, I MUST FINISH BY ACTING."
-HENRY DAVID THOREAU

The days went by rapidly, one chasing the next as I rose early to head out to my work at the Library. My duties there, had I listed them out, would appear of no special import to someone perusing the list but, to me, represented my being a part, albeit small, of a very significant community event. That frame of mind transformed hours spent on clerical tasks and running errands for the assistant librarian from what might otherwise be seen as tedious, unchallenging activity into an important "mission."

Late one afternoon, realizing that I had lost track of time and would have to hurry so as not to be late for supper, I came quickly down the center stairs from the second floor to encounter Andrew Pritchard in the front foyer of the Library. With that supper was forgotten as, for me, time had effectively stopped. Some pleasantries were exchanged, Andrew saying that he had come in to borrow a newly-published book on the topic of modern accounting principles. What would normally be a very dry topic in my eyes somehow sounded terribly interesting to ears that took in the words delivered by the appealing tones of his voice. The less appealing voice of the assistant head librarian bidding me a "good evening" as she left the building restarted the passage of time and I remembered the awaiting supper at home. With great regret I began to excuse myself only to have Andrew offer to walk me home. He said that spending hours and days sitting behind a desk, he had made it a habit to "stretch" his legs with regular walks lest those limbs wither or his knees seize up in protest at being so long in one daily position. Mrs. Boone, in "lookout" stance on the front porch, saw us as we approached the house. I parted my lips to begin my apology for being late but was interdicted by instruction for both Andrew and me to come inside as the meal was soon to be on the table. That announcement was accompanied by a slight tilt of her head in my direction and the now familiar conspiratorial lifting of her eyebrows.

Looking back, I now realize that I chattered through both the walk home with Andrew and supper, mostly talking about the Library . . . and topics centering on *me*. Now a cringe-worthy memory, I so clearly see the tell-tale signs of my self-absorbed immaturity working in concert with my overwhelming desire to make myself appealing to Andrew. Mercifully, a better heart prevailed in the form of Mrs. Boone. She inquired about Andrew's work for Mr. Gatling and then, with unobtrusive delicacy, asked about his family. His response to the inquiry about his family came slowly. He was born near Roanoke he said but no longer had any family there. In fact, he no longer had any family anywhere. Mrs. Boone's face lost color as she struggled with feelings of compassion for Andrew and guilt for having put him in the position of having to talk about such a personal thing.

Once daring to lift the lid on his family history, he went on to tell us that his mother had died in childbirth when his younger sister was born. His father, who had "adored" his mother was laid very low by her death and it fell to Andrew's maternal grandparents to take on the care of Andrew and the new baby girl. Andrew's grandfather was a veteran of the war who had purchased a small plot of land thereafter upon which he built a cabin for himself and his bride. They farmed their little property, lived off that land and sold their excess to make a small income. Andrew smiled warmly as he described their marriage partnership, fused in love, mutual respect, and common purpose. Andrew and his sister were well-loved and provided for in that modest home. Despite his grandparents' repeated efforts to console Andrew's father and offer him their support, he kept himself alone, consumed with mourning his wife and consoled only by the alcohol that robbed him of his health and, in the end, his very life. Andrew's grandparents, by then his "parents," had both passed away by the time he was twelve and his sister seven and, through the kindness of a local minister, they were placed in an orphanage in Roanoke where they received more than passable care and a decent education.

When Andrew paused, Mrs. Boone excused herself for a moment to bring in a tray with tea and some oatmeal cookies she had made earlier that day. When she sat again, her eyes met Andrew's, both sets of eyes shadowed with loss but faintly lit with unspoken mutual consolation. I wanted to let Andrew know that I too "understood" by telling him about Luke, my parents, and the lost unborn babies but I had not yet mastered my sorrow as they had and I could not find the words. But, having been listening so raptly, I was suddenly curious about Andrew's sister. She had been in the orphanage with him yet he started by saying he had "no family" left in this world. Yes, I asked. Mrs. Boone shot me a look very different from the one with conspiratorial raised eyebrows. Her eyes wide as saucers, it conveyed her shock at my insensitivity. As the cups of tea went untouched and cold, Andrew explained that his sister had died just a year earlier, a victim of consumption. He exhaled and picked up a cookie and put it in his mouth. Fresh tea was served and not long after that he left, graciously thanking us for supper.

I received a much-needed *explanation* (I could not call it a *lecture* or *talking-to* as Mrs. Boone was too kind even in her admonishments to warrant those terms) of my "surely unintended" missteps during the supper conversation. Recognizing that I was still finding my way from "girl" to "woman," she mostly excused my behavior as a consequence of immaturity. In fact, as she later told me, she took my seeming insensitivity as indication that I had not yet come to terms with my own loss, a means of insulating myself against that pain and sorrow. At the time, I had asked if she felt guilty herself for having asked Andrew about his family. She said she had and initially wished that she could call back her words even at the cost of choking on them but, seeing and hearing

Andrew offer so much more than would be required in polite response, she later thought differently. She wondered if sharing the story was in some fashion cathartic for him not unlike the way that disposing of a nagging secret lifts a burden from the one who had been keeping it. I hoped that might be the case and Andrew was none-the-worse for those revelations.

I worried that the goings-on at supper would create a rift between Andrew and me . . . and Mrs. Boone. Had we crossed a line and barged in where we had no right to be? Would we be excused for what happened due to the innocence that caused it? Having bared himself to me and Mrs. Boone, would a sense of embarrassment on his part serve to make him distance himself from us? Those questions were answered less than a week later when Andrew came to the house one evening. He arrived unexpected at about 8:00 as Mrs. Boone and I sat reading, each in our favorite parlor chair. I rose and opened the door to find Andrew. I asked him to come in. He came into the parlor but did not sit as we offered. From his jacket pocket he withdrew what appeared to be tickets of some kind. He explained that Miss Eugenie Blair, a well-known actress and Richmond native, was coming to the American Theatre here in Norfolk for a two-day engagement in her popular role as "Madame X." He had procured three tickets and invited me and Mrs. Boone to join him for the play that following Thursday evening. I wanted to immediately say "yes" but, knowing Mrs. Boone was not one usually found in a theatre, I stifled my response and looked at her. When she delayed in answering, Andrew offered a bit of information about the story which was billed as "a great mother-love drama." That was enough to pique her interest and, accepting, she thanked Andrew for his kindness. After he left, I commented to Mrs. Boone that Andrew had come at an hour rather later than usual for a visitor. Mrs. Boone, never looking up from her book, replied matter-of-factly that it was the perfect time to arrive without risking an invitation to stay for a meal. It was then that I concluded that Mrs. Boone's quiet, unassuming exterior obviously concealed a creature part each psychic, prophet, and philosopher.

When Thursday finally arrived, my stomach was fluttering as I watched the clock slowly make its circuit through the hours until 4:00 when I hurried home from the Library for a light meal with Mrs. Boone. After picking at my food while continuing my clock-watching from the dining table, I excused myself and darted off to dress and redo my hair. I put on my graduation dress, pale green textured silk with a short matching jacket. I went to my small jewelry casket and found the worn velvet pouch containing the small strand of pearls that Father had given Mother as an anniversary gift.

My memory called up a scene when I was a little girl and had asked Mother to let me wear the pearl necklace. She briefly draped it around my tiny neck and told me that one day the pearls would be mine which made me very happy. How could I have ever imagined that the passing of the ownership of the pearls from Mother to me would come at the cost of losing her? I quickly fastened the pearls as Mrs. Boone called to me saying it was time to leave for the theatre.

Andrew was waiting for us near the box office standing alongside a poster picturing Miss Eugenie Blair. He handed in our tickets and escorted us to our seats – very fine seats in the center section of the theatre not more than ten rows from the stage. The deep burgundy velvet stage curtains, trimmed in luxurious sparkling gold rope, were still closed and there were musicians tuning up in the small orchestra pit in anticipation of the start of the program.

I had purchased a copy of the *Richmond Times Dispatch* after hearing that there was a feature article recounting an interview with Miss Blair. Having read the article beginning to end (twice), I felt very well acquainted with the woman soon to rule the stage as "Madame X." Miss Blair, although not actually born in Richmond herself, was the daughter of Charles Blair and Ella Wren who married in Richmond during the war. Ella, a young actress performing with the Richmond Theatre Stock Company was born in England and, according to the newspaper article, was quite a beauty as well as being a "versatile" actress who performed in comedy, drama, and even operatic roles. Ella met her future husband when he was serving as provost marshal in Richmond. Miss Blair told the reporter that she herself was "nearly born on the stage" and suspected she developed her interest in acting in her early years while accompanying her mother to her performances. She talked about the talented people she was working with and the challenge of pleasing the audience. I could hardly sit still until the curtain went up.

Eugenie Blair gave a bravura performance as "Madame X," a woman who made a mistake when young and paid dearly for it at the hands of her embittered husband who deprived her of her child as the ultimate punishment for her sin. As the applause died down we rose and joined the crowd slowly exiting the theatre. Andrew asked how we enjoyed the play and I began telling him and Mrs. Boone all about Miss Blair, her ties to Virginia, and the different roles she had performed. At one point when I took a much-needed breath, Mrs. Boone told Andrew that she had never before seen a professional play and that the story, while a bit frank with reference to the "sin" that was the cause of the tragic separation of mother and child, was performed with great sincerity. Andrew walked us home and came in for a cup of tea and a slice of apple spice cake. We thanked him again as he rose to leave and reiterated what fun it had been to have a night out at the theatre. As my head lay on the pillow that night, the unopened (and barely read) copy of *The Scarlet Letter* on my bedside table, I thought of Madame X and Hester Prynne, both of them women whose motherhood defined their tragic lives. I promised myself that, despite the archaic language that made the book such a challenge for me to read, I would make a better effort to do so.

My growing infatuation with Andrew took the form of daydreams and moments when, quite conscious, my mind was full of thoughts of places we would go and things we would share. My next birthday was not that many months away and I thought, on that occasion, we might once again go to the theatre – just the two of us this time. He would offer me his arm as we strolled down Granby Street toward the American Theatre and people would notice what a splendid couple we made. The day after our outing to see Eugenie Blair in "Madame X," I asked Mrs. Boone if, in addition to having told Andrew how much we enjoyed the play, it would be appropriate to write him a personal note expressing our thanks. She thought that a very nice idea saying that while "modern" society had begun to take on a new "informality" of manners, she preferred the niceties of her upbringing, extra effort notwithstanding. I penned a short note (in my best feminine hand) and signed it on behalf of myself and Mrs. Boone and, of course, intended to deliver it myself. Although my plan was to go to Mr. Gatling's office to give the note to Andrew, it occurred to me that I had never asked Andrew where he lived and so did not know his address had I wanted to mail the thank you note instead. I would talk less and listen more in the future I promised myself.

A day later on my way home from the Library I went to Mr. Gatling's office to deliver the note. I entered but Andrew was not at his desk. Mr. Coates, the head bookkeeper, looked up and greeted me politely. I asked for Andrew, thinking I had come too late and he had gone for the day. Mr. Coates looked a bit confused at my inquiry but before he could respond Mr. Gatling came out of his office apparently about to leave for home. I restated for him that I had come to see Mr. Pritchard. Mr. Gatling asked if my inquiry was in reference to my account as, if so, Mr. Coates or one of the other clerks would be happy to assist. Something suddenly felt *wrong* and it must have shown on my face. I recall Mr. Gatling saying something about my having had a "long day" at the Library and ushering me into his office so I could sit down and explain what I needed. After that my recollections of the particulars of our conversation are vague. The import of it is etched into my brain: Andrew Pritchard had completed his apprenticeship with Mr. Gatling and had gone home to Roanoke to be married in two weeks. In the mere minutes between my initial inquiry about Andrew to Mr. Coates and Mr. Gatling's announcement about Andrew's pending marriage, a thought that he had been hurt or even killed had flashed through my mind. In fact, Andrew Pritchard was "dead" to me. The cause? Matrimony.

I am not sure how but I drank a few sips of the water Mr. Gatling had put in front of me (I expect I looked a sudden sickly color) and said my question was related to the expense ledger Mr. Pritchard had prepared but was of no real consequence, just a small curiosity. Promising to make an appointment with Mr. Coates should I need to revisit it, I bid the gentlemen in the office good evening and slowly walked home. My insides were churning, as feelings of sorrow and disappointment battled those of anger and betrayal. My anger, sharp as a knife blade, was winning the contest and banished the tears that my sorrow wanted to set free. My cheeks were dry as the desert when I arrived home, crimson and burning once again but not from schoolgirl embarrassment as in the past. They were hot with the knowledge that I had misjudged Andrew Pritchard's character and he had played me false.

When I reached out to grasp the front door latch, I found my right hand was still gripping the envelope containing the thank you note. I loosed my rage on that small paper emblem of my foolishness, ripping it into small pieces that fell at my feet. I did not stoop to pick up the remains of the note. I went into the house and straight to my room, doors flying closed behind me. Mrs. Boone, who no doubt heard the sound of slamming doors, soon knocked on my bedroom door asking if she could come in. Knowing I would have to tell her sooner or later, I said she should come in. Misery does love to have company and I was sure she would be appalled at how I had been misused by Andrew. Misery may seek like partners but Mrs. Boone's temperate reaction to the news of Andrew's impending marriage did not make her equal to that role and instead put some salt squarely into my righteous wound. I thought about how I had wanted to tell Andrew about my loss of all my family and had chastised myself for my inability to talk to him about it. Now I was so glad I had not done so. He had proved himself unworthy of my trust.

I seethed for days, unwilling to be consoled or reasoned with. It would take a good two weeks and a church sermon I swore Mrs. Boone had requested specifically for my benefit, but my anger waned sufficiently that I could admit that Mrs. Boone's view of what had happened was more measured and even-handed than mine. She took me back through the time we spent with Andrew, step-by-step, putting the few meals we shared and the theatre invitation into context. I first crossed paths with Andrew at Mr. Gatling's office, his workplace. Taken with him, I returned there on a pretext hoping to see him again. I assumed that his bringing the expense ledger to the house was done as a pretext to see me and impress me with his thoughtfulness. Perhaps I should not have equated his motive to mine . . . perhaps it was nothing but thoughtfulness. When I ran into him at the Library and he walked me home, I believed it another sign of his wanting to see me. Maybe it was an accidental crossing of paths and his purpose in walking home with me was simply to "stretch" his legs while courteously keeping me company. Both times he ate with us, it was unplanned and the result of an invitation from Mrs. Boone that he likely felt would be rude to refuse. And then there was the outing to the theatre, an opportunity for him to repay my and Mrs. Boone's kindness knowing he would soon be leaving Norfolk for Roanoke. Righteous indignation drained out of me and my mood lifted . . . finally. The one thing I was not ready to do was to wish Andrew well in his marriage even if Mrs. Boone was so disposed but I could not deny her observation that he had endured a great deal to get to a chance at family and happiness once again.

My work at the Library helped me to move on and divert my thoughts away from Andrew and his new life. The search for a site to be home to the new branch was underway as were discussions as to whether to buy an existing building for conversion or a parcel on which a new building would be constructed. Long lists of possibilities were being pared down to short lists of final candidates in each category for in-depth consideration. I was kept busy in my role as administrative clerk, project intermediary, and general "assistant," all roles I usually enjoyed.

I hadn't seen as much of Miss Isobel, my preoccupation with Andrew and busy work days at the Library filling my time. She deserved better from me. I did notice that she had not been much at the Library recently and promised myself I would arrange to go see her soon. I hoped she would not ask me how my reading of *The Scarlet Letter* was progressing as it was not. I also hoped that she was not aware of the debacle with Andrew Pritchard though I reasoned that Mr. Gatling may have suspected what had happened and, if so, could have told her.

The next Sunday afternoon I went to see Miss Isobel. I should have sent her a note first to confirm a convenient time for my visit but, anxious to see her, I just went over to her house unannounced. At worst, she would be out or unable to see me because she was entertaining other visitors. At least, if either were the case, I would be able to talk with Katie, ask how Miss Isobel was, and confirm when I might come back to see her. I rang the bell and instead of Katie, a strange young woman opened the door. I gave her my name and asked to see Miss Isobel or Katie. She admitted me to the foyer and said I should wait there. It was several minutes before Katie came down the stairs. At first glance, she appeared tired and her smile forced.

She motioned for me to follow her into kitchen where she washed her hands and began making a pot of tea. As we waited for the water to come to a boil, she sat with me at the small kitchen table. She told me that Miss Isobel had been ill for over a week and was upstairs resting in bed. She had come down sick with cough and congestion after a day out with friends, insisted "it would pass" and that there was no need to call for Dr. Heath. She developed a mild fever that persisted and then went up alarmingly. On the fourth day, Katie went to her in the morning and she was speaking "nonsense" and unable to respond sensibly to Katie's questions. At that point Katie, afraid to leave Miss Isobel even to go the few blocks to summon Dr. Heath, instead asked a neighbor boy to hurry there and tell the doctor it was urgent that he come to Miss Isobel. Dr. Heath, a very capable physician and one of the doctors who had tried so hard to save my father, came quickly and diagnosed Miss Isobel with a severe case of the grippe. He prescribed some tonics and absolute bed rest and had been checking in on her daily since then. Seeing that Katie obviously needed help with Miss Isobel's care (and at least several hours of decent sleep), he arranged for a nursing student to stay at the house. That was the young woman who answered the door when I rang.

I knew I shouldn't but I asked if I could see Miss Isobel. While she was better than she had been a few days earlier, she was still very weak. Katie said she had been sleeping when I arrived. She suggested that we have a cup of tea after which she would check and see if Miss Isobel was then awake. If she was, Katie would ask if I could sit by her bedside and visit for just a few minutes. As I drank my tea, I wished that Miss Isobel would be awake when Katie checked on her. More than that, I wished I had visited sooner and known she was so very ill. As it turned out, Miss Isobel was still sleeping when Katie checked on her after we had our tea. She let me come upstairs and peek into her room for a few moments. Covered up to her chin with a lovely floral quilt, she looked so small and pale but she was breathing softly and did not appear in any discomfort. I thanked God she was recovering. Before leaving I offered to stay at the house to help until Miss Isobel was stronger. Katie said the crisis was over and it was now just a matter of rest and getting Miss Isobel's appetite back but thanked me for my offer. I asked if I could come back after work the next day and Katie said "of course." As I made my way home, any thoughts other than those about Miss Isobel disappeared from my mind, no longer mattering to me. Uncharacteristically for me, I could not hold back tears when I told Mrs. Boone about Miss Isobel and I found that letting the tears come was unexpectedly soothing.

Part Two: Izzy

"Death was too definite an object to be wished for or avoided."

~Nathaniel Hawthorne (*The Scarlet Letter*)

EIGHT: "TIME FLIES OVER US, BUT LEAVES ITS SHADOW BEHIND."
-NATHANIEL HAWTHORNE

Week by passing week Miss Isobel got stronger and seemed her old self although she would sometimes get a sudden spell of coughing that would then pass in a short time. She was often at the Library and worked with me on the new branch project. A property located in Ocean View had been purchased for the new branch and an Alexandria architectural firm retained to draw up plans for the new building. On a brisk November day I accompanied Miss Isobel to Alexandria for a meeting with the architect. She would be representing the Library Board and Mr. Sargeant, head of the Library, relaying comments and suggestions resulting from their review of the first draft of the building plans. She had a leather portfolio crammed full with her detailed notes along with a marked-up copy of the plans. We had booked passage through the Norfolk and Washington Steamboat Company and sailed to Alexandria on the beautiful steamer *Newport News*.

My excitement was at fever pitch as I packed for the four-day trip. I had never been on a boat like the *Newport News* but had seen posters and descriptions of such luxury steamers. Mrs. Boone was almost as excited as I was and fussed about trying to make sure I had everything I needed. Not only had I never traveled by steamer, I had never been to a city as historic and important as Alexandria. This was going to be the highlight of my life, no question about it. I was almost bursting with anticipation when the morning of our departure finally came.

Mrs. Boone saw us off at the dock waving furiously as the steamer pulled away. Miss Isobel showed me around and I was amazed to see the fine sitting areas, dining facilities, and other amenities. We had two meals on board, each so delicious and beautifully served. Miss Isobel had made arrangements for two adjoining rooms at a lovely hotel in the most historic area of Alexandria. After our long day, we unpacked and shared a small meal in our rooms. By then, worn out by my excitement and the long trip on the steamer, I went to bed and was fast asleep in no time.

Watching Miss Isobel interact with the architect the next day, exchanging thoughts and ideas and resolving potential problems and issues was so very interesting. She represented Mr. Sargeant and the board admirably and I saw the respect with which the architect entertained her suggestions and questions. Discussions and negotiations completed, we packed up the leather portfolio and were soon on our way back to the hotel. Miss Isobel had a surprise for me. We were going to have an early supper at our hotel and then would be off to the Washington Street Methodist Episcopal Church to attend a lecture to be given by Dr. Sam A. Steel, a preacher, editor, and well-known orator. A friend of Mr. Sargeant's had kindly provided the tickets to the lecture. Dr. Steel was known for his talks about life in the South during the war, drawing large audiences to hear his reminiscences. Miss Isobel knew I was fond of the study of history and said she thought I would enjoy Dr. Steel's program titled "Home Life in Dixie During the War" as the topic would include his recollections of everyday life during the four years of the war. She said she understood the talk was historically instructive but also included the retelling of humorous situations as well.

We arrived at the church, handed in our tickets and were ushered to our seats. Judging by the crowd outside, the lecture would be very well attended. Our seats were near the podium and I was sure we would feel the full force of Dr. Steel's presentation. As seats were filled, an elegant elderly woman and a younger woman, perhaps her daughter, were seated next to us, the older woman next to me. I looked over and smiled politely at them and they returned the smile. Miss Isobel was conversing with a dapper gentleman sitting next to her and I thought they made a handsome couple. In anticipation of the start of the program, some of the lighting was turned down making the well-lit podium area the focal point of the room. All eyes would be on Dr. Steel.

Dr. Steel was introduced to enthusiastic applause. He began by thanking the leaders of the church for having him, said he had come to Alexandria directly from an engagement at Cornell University, and was extremely glad to be once again "home in the

South." He then thanked Mrs. Melanie Ward for her hospitality in having him as her house guest while he was visiting Alexandria, gesturing in the direction of the elegant lady sitting next to me. I heard Miss Isobel make a small sound of surprise as her head turned to look past me and toward the woman who I now knew was Mrs. Ward. Half under her breath, I heard Miss Isobel say "Mellie?" Mrs. Ward may have been a woman of considerable years but her ears were apparently still in fine working condition and she leaned forward in response to the hardly audible sound of her name. In the dimmed light, both women tilted their heads looking past me in the direction of each other. There was recognition in both faces but not a reaction that would indicate the unexpected discovery of a dear friend or relative. Instead, something like a polite nod was exchanged from either side of me. At that point, Dr. Steel's voice echoed from the podium and both women sat back in their chairs, eyes forward and focused on him.

The program paused for a short intermission after forty-five minutes, no doubt to allow Dr. Steel a short respite and a drink of water or some other beverage. Even before the lights came up, Mrs. Ward and her companion stood and moved into the center aisle following other attendees into a central lobby where people began to mingle in small groups. Miss Isobel and I waited for the crowd to thin and then made our way up the aisle to the lobby. I saw Mrs. Ward across the room engaged in a lively conversation with several people and wondered if Miss Isobel would approach her but did not dare ask. Miss Isobel asked if I might need to use the powder room and, thinking that a good idea, we did so together. When we returned to the lobby, Mrs. Ward came walking toward us. Miss Isobel greeted her in a reserved but cordial manner and introduced me. Mrs. Ward then inquired about our being in Alexandria. Miss Isobel explained the purpose of our trip and Mrs. Ward looked over at me and asked if it was my first visit there. I responded with an enthusiastic "yes" continuing on to say how wonderful it was to come to such a fine city with so much history. At that point the announcement was made that we should all return to our seats for part two of Dr. Steel's talk and we proceeded back to our seats followed by Mrs. Ward.

Dr. Steel was a most animated speaker and quite a storyteller so much so that his words provoked mental images that drew one into the story he was telling. I was most entertained by his program and was a bit sorry when he concluded his lecture to a standing ovation from those in attendance. When the lights came up once again, Mrs. Ward turned to us. Patting my hand gently, she looked at Miss Isobel and coolly extended a dinner invitation for the following evening. She said Dr. Steel and some others would be there. I looked hopefully at Miss Isobel. The invitation was accepted and we were to be at Mrs. Ward's home on South Washington Street promptly at seven-thirty. With a restrained "good night" offered to each other, Mrs. Ward and Miss Isobel said no more. My curiosity was boiling over but I thought it best not to ask any questions about Mrs. Ward until the next day when we would be doing some touring of the historic sites of the city.

After breakfast we set off strolling beautiful King Street. I was fascinated with the gracious old homes and classic architecture. We visited Alexandria City Hall on which site more than a century earlier there had been a bustling city market. The three-story brick building, originally built in 1817, included a clock tower that became a famous landmark in the city. The clock tower was designed by Benjamin Henry Latrobe, one of the architects of the U.S. Capitol. In 1871, a tremendous fire left the building severely damaged. The citizens of Alexandria, determined to have the building rebuilt, raised the funds necessary to have that done, including a replica of Latrobe's clock tower.

After a pleasant mid-day meal at a café on King Street, Miss Isobel said she had another surprise for me: we were going to George Washington's home, Mount Vernon. I hugged her, nearly squeezing all the breath out of her lungs. We traveled to Mount Vernon on the electric streetcar line of the Washington, Alexandria, & Mount Vernon Railroad. When the magnificent white house with its circular drive and expansive lawn came into view my breath caught at the sight of it. I threaded my arm through Miss Isobel's and we walked toward the door to register for a tour of the house. The Mount Vernon Ladies Association, formed by a group of women dedicated to the preservation of Washington's home, agreed to purchase Mount Vernon in 1858 at a cost of $200,000. The house was then in quite a state of disrepair ("dilapidation" some had described it at the time) and, in the five decades since then, the Mount Vernon ladies had tirelessly raised funds for the restoration of the house to its original historic condition representing the way it was when occupied by George and Martha Washington. Beyond the restoration of the house and gardens, they set upon acquiring original period furnishings, including articles belonging to the Washington family.

I could have stayed in the house for hours and hours, there was so much to see. Just to think that we walked where President Washington walked was difficult to believe. The grounds were beautifully manicured and the view of the Potomac from the columned porch was exceptional. To say it was "picturesque" would not do it justice. Too soon it was time to catch the streetcar back to Alexandria so we could dress for dinner at Mrs. Ward's home. I thanked Miss Isobel for such a wonderful excursion and I promised myself that I would return to Mount Vernon one day.

Needless to say, the day of sightseeing in Alexandria and visiting Mount Vernon was so wonderful (and completely absorbing) that I had all but forgotten my previously pressing curiosity to hear more about the history between Miss Isobel and Mrs. Ward. Might some of my questions be answered at the dinner at Mrs. Ward's home? If not, I resolved I would take the risk and ask Miss Isobel during our trip home on the steamer.

We arrived promptly at seven-thirty. Mrs. Ward's home was a stately three-story house of muted red brick with Greek Revival elements and fourteen shuttered windows gracing the front façade. Although a city house, it was surrounded by more than ample grounds on both sides and in the rear. The front door opened into a spacious foyer with a center hallway and an archway leading to a staircase that curved and stretched upward to the second floor. The hall was lit by a sparkling crystal chandelier suspended from the vaulted ceiling above. I could hear animated voices and laughter as we entered the house and our coats were taken. We were shown to a large parlor where guests were mingling as they enjoyed a drink before dinner. I tried to take in the breadth of the parlor without appearing to gawk.

My first impression was that the room spoke of a person whose tastes were influenced by the Far East. The furnishings were not the latest in modern taste but had the sensibility of being favorite pieces grouped to show them to their best advantage and to convey a feeling of warmth and comfort in the room. There were two stunning oriental carpets in shades of blue and cream covering the floor. Among the pieces that I found most lovely were a pair of matching tête-a-têtes that faced each other in front of the elegant fireplace. On the mantle were matching antique brass and crystal girandoles on either side of a large figurine of a woman under a glass dome that appeared to be carved jade. Over the fireplace was a painting of an early nineteenth century sailing ship with three masts under which was a gift inscription and the date 1859. In the corner my eye discovered something most unexpected: a large ornate domed gilt metal cage on a stand occupied by an exotic multicolor bird, a parrot I believe. Apparently uninterested in and unbothered by the noise and goings-on in the parlor, the bird was happily feasting on a small and no doubt tasty wedge of apple.

A call to adjourn to the dining room came quickly thereafter and we made our way to the long, carved dining table that comfortably sat all twenty or so guests. The matching sideboard was host to an impressive hand-painted Chinese vase filled with fresh flowers in a rainbow of colors flanked on either side by twin antique mahogany boxes that I suspected held silver flatware. Above the veined white marble fireplace hung a huge gilt mirror and on the mantle below it were a most unusual old clock with a music box at its base and a half dozen small photographs in ornate silver and gold frames. Looking at the wall opposite the fireplace, I was surprised to see three oval carved wood frames holding portrait engravings of Confederate Generals Johnson, Jackson, and Lee. As in the parlor, the windows were dressed with lace curtains that gracefully fell to the floor from under cornices made of brass, something I had never seen before. I thought the fine china dinnerware almost too beautiful to eat on lest the decoration of petite plumed birds and gilt be marred by utensils. The meal, many courses long, was thoroughly delicious even though I was not always sure what some of the dishes were.

Dr. Steel entertained us with his reminiscences and tales as we ate and the mood was jovial and enjoyable in every way. As we savored the dessert course and there was a lull in the conversing (being full to the brim will eventually slow even lively people down a bit), I was able to speak to Dr. Steel and tell him how much I enjoyed his lecture of the night before. I said I hoped he might come to Norfolk someday as I was sure that crowds of attendees would queue up to see him and hear his talks. He listened attentively and very graciously thanked me. The evening's activities completed, Miss Isobel and I once again thanked Mrs. Ward for having us and were soon back at our hotel. The next morning we would have an early breakfast at the hotel and then get to the dock to board the steamer that would return us to Norfolk.

The weather had been perfect during our trip but it had begun to rain as we went onboard the steamer. We made our way to the salon and found some comfortable overstuffed chairs in a private corner of the room. Miss Isobel ordered a pot of tea and two assorted fruit plates and we settled in for the "voyage" home to Norfolk. Sipping tea and nibbling on orange sections, peach slices, and strawberries, we relived the events of the last two days, especially the afternoon at Mount Vernon. I told Miss Isobel that it was the best of surprises and thanked her again most sincerely. I was so looking forward to telling Mrs. Boone all about it – every bit I could remember. When the tea tray and plates were taken away and we sat back relaxing, I knew it was *now or never* if I meant to ask about Mrs. Ward and her ties to Miss Isobel.

I prefaced by saying that I "did not mean to pry." After that statement, came the inevitable "but" that effectively made mincemeat of my assertion that I hadn't intended to stick my nose where it didn't belong. Nose so occupied, my mouth opened again and out came the first of my many questions, my initial inquiry throwing out a rather wide net. I asked how Miss Isobel came to know Mrs. Ward. Miss Isobel sighed, was silent for a few moments and then, after mulling things over, said it was a "long story." I replied that we had nothing but a dreary day and hours on the water ahead of us so the telling of a "long story" would be just the thing for passing the time.

Melanie Husted Ward was born in Portsmouth, New Hampshire. She was the daughter of a very successful sea captain who often sailed to the Far East as part of what was called "the China trade." The Captain commanded a number of clipper ships over his career as a mariner and transported both goods and people to and from New England, California, China, and India, some of those "people" being Chinese indentured workers often referred to disparagingly as "coolies."

Melanie, her mother, and brother Philip sometimes traveled with him on these extended voyages to the other side of the world and, when old enough, Philip became his father's first mate. Returning from one such trip, the ship made port for a short stay in Alexandria so the Husteds might avail themselves of the social opportunities of the city. It was in Alexandria that Melanie met her future husband, Randall Laird Ward, a Virginia native and successful dry goods merchant. A romance and courtship soon followed and the couple were married in New York City not long after. Captain Husted, obviously approving of the match, gave his daughter and her new husband the gift of the house on South Washington Street where Miss Isobel and I had been to dinner.

Stating the obvious, I commented that Mrs. Ward had lived in that fine house for many years to which Miss Isobel answered "more than a half century." My mind was hard at work taking in the story thus far and queuing up questions I wanted to ask Miss Isobel. I was also trying to reconcile Mrs. Ward being a born and bred New Englander and "Yankee" transplant to Virginia with the framed engravings of the three Confederate generals so conspicuously displayed in her dining room.

I don't know how long I was staring off contemplating that conundrum when I heard Miss Isobel say my name. She pointed out that it was past noon and since we had a very early breakfast it was time we got something to eat. Realizing I was hungry, I agreed but made her promise to continue the story after we ate. I had learned a lot about Mrs. Ward and her family but I still didn't know how she and Miss Isobel came to know each other and how they later became estranged.

NINE: "NO TWO PERSONS EVER READ THE SAME BOOK."
-EDMUND WILSON

I cleaned my plate and waited somewhat impatiently for Miss Isobel to do the same. Finally we returned to our quiet corner of the salon where the tea Miss Isobel had ordered was brought over along with a few sweets to go with it. Miss Isobel poured the tea ever so slowly and I realized she was teasing me by doing so. She daintily lifted the fine china cup to her lips and sipped, returning the cup to its saucer languidly. I couldn't help myself. I asked again how she met Mrs. Ward to get the story going. With a devilish grin Miss Isobel responded, saying that there was a good deal more to tell before getting to that part of the story.

Not long after Melanie Husted married Randall Ward and they settled in their new home in Alexandria, tragedy came to call when Melanie's father Captain Husted and her brother Philip each died. Philip, on a voyage with and serving under his father, was killed during a mutiny at sea. Just months later, Captain Husted fell suddenly ill as his ship was preparing to dock in Cuba and he died in Havana.

Those losses were followed in short order by the outbreak of the war in 1861. Mrs. Ward was a young wife and mother to two small daughters when the Union Army crossed the Potomac River and quickly occupied Arlington and then Alexandria. In fact, it was in Alexandria that the first Union officer met his death. Colonel Elmer Ellsworth, a young man who led a Union regiment from New York, had arrived at the Alexandria docks with his troops by steamer. As Ellsworth and his men made their way through the town to secure it for the Union, he spotted a large Confederate flag flying from the roof of a local inn. Ellsworth halted, determined to take down the offending flag that was so large it was visible from Washington, DC. He entered the inn with a few of his men, made his way to the roof and tore down the flag. On his way down the stairs he encountered the innkeeper James Jackson, an ardent secessionist, who fired his shotgun fatally wounding Ellsworth. The innkeeper was killed instantly, shot by one of the Union soldiers accompanying Ellsworth. Colonel Ellsworth was apparently well-known to Abraham Lincoln and it was arranged that Ellsworth's body lay in state at the White House, making him a martyr for the Union cause. The innkeeper was likewise held up as a martyr – for the Confederacy.

The war years brought oppressive Union occupations and martial law to many areas of the South, including Alexandria. The occupation remade Alexandria, changing a tranquil and stately mid-sized port city into a beehive of Union Army support activity. The majority of Alexandrians who were not away fighting for the

Confederacy abandoned the city and those who stayed lived under military rules and scrutiny. Homes were invaded and searched by Union troops and were summarily appropriated for occupation by officers, repurposing as barracks for enlisted men or for use as hospitals. Most objectionable was the Union Army interference in community religious services and their humiliation of local ministers. Perversely, the early and continued occupation of Alexandria did, however, largely save the city from the more destructive effects of battling forces and armament.

After the war, Mr. Ward restarted his business in earnest operating his dry goods enterprise on King Street where he offered a wide assortment of fine fabrics for dresses, household linens, and sundries for both men and women. He was a leader in the local mercantile businessmen's organization and active in local community affairs including the Masons. He also was employed as an insurance agent and a realtor in Alexandria and had opened a dry goods sample store in Washington, DC. He and Mrs. Ward and their children were once again living a prosperous, happy life.

But it was not to last. Heartache visited Mrs. Ward again a decade later when her husband Randall died in a railroad accident while traveling through the Shenandoah Valley of Virginia. Randall Ward, then forty-five years old, was a passenger on a train mostly comprised of cars full of livestock and carrying only about twenty male passengers, mostly all men who had an ownership interest in the stock being transported. Near midnight, the train entered upon the Narrow Passage Bridge, a span of some two hundred feet long at a height of over one hundred feet above a deep, narrow ravine formed by two very steep precipices. As the ill-fated train reached the middle of the bridge, the structure gave way with about a hundred feet of it falling into the ravine below. With that collapse, the train cars followed, tumbling into the gorge in an enormous pile of twisted metal and debris. Newspaper reports said that the bridge had been burned during the war and was rebuilt after the end of that conflict, locals claiming it was not well done. At the time of the accident, the bridge was undergoing construction activity to install new supports and strengthen the structure. Randall Ward, along with ten other men, perished in the catastrophic accident, his lifeless body having been brought home in the care of his Mason brothers.

Miss Isobel recalled reading the ghastly descriptions of the calamity in newspapers of the day, the stories going so far as to describe the specific nature of the victims' injuries in unseemly detail. While Miss Isobel, then a young woman in her early twenties, was one of the many Virginians who read about the train disaster and the eleven men who died as a result, she was not yet acquainted with Mrs. Ward. Only when the two women met through mutual friends fully a decade later would Miss Isobel find out about Mrs. Ward's tragic connection to that railroad catastrophe. Their introduction came by way of C.C. Gatling and his wife Belinda. Belinda had been born in Alexandria and lived very near Mrs. Ward on South Washington Street until the age of twelve when her family moved to Norfolk.

Now I knew how they met but that still left the question of what had caused the obvious coolness and distance between them. In for a penny, in for a pound, as the old saying goes. I asked. Miss Isobel shook her finger at me in a mock scolding manner and said I was a more "curious cat" than even the nosiest feline she had ever encountered but, to my relief, she did continue the story.

Miss Isobel and C.C. Gatling had known each other since they were about ten years old. Belinda had come to Norfolk a few years later and had been in school with them. Belinda was a sweet girl with very pale skin, fine wispy brown hair, and small brown eyes that defined her as "plain" and even perhaps sickly. She also had a natural shyness that made her transition to a new community and school a difficult task for her. Miss Isobel hadn't forgotten when she was new to Norfolk some years earlier at the time she and her mother took up residence there. She remembered that rascal C.C. Gatling teasing her when she was the new girl in class, his tomfoolery culminating in a tug on her hair that was met with the resounding sound of her small hand slapping his face. From that day forth they were the best of friends despite more episodes of teasing, tugging, and other shenanigans as the years went by.

Miss Isobel and Mr. Gatling "adopted" Belinda and a twosome of best friends soon became a threesome. As the three adolescents came of age, it was obvious to Miss Isobel that Belinda was enamored of Mr. Gatling although he showed not the smallest sign of seeing that or having reciprocal feelings for Belinda. In fact, people often observed that he was "sweet on" Miss Isobel.

Whether because she believed that or just as a consequence of her shyness, Belinda never expressed her feelings to Mr. Gatling. Miss Isobel did mention it to him at the time that she and Belinda were going off to boarding school when they were about sixteen. Young Mr. Gatling, a bit red-faced, dismissed it as a "silly schoolgirl thing" that would "pass," especially with Belinda's time at school. He was quite wrong. Two years away at school did little to alter Belinda's feelings. The young woman of eighteen who returned home after graduation was more poised and self-aware and was even more sure of her love for him.

Belinda remained patient and faithful to her feelings without imposing herself on Mr. Gatling as anything other than a friend. The years went by in that way, with neither Belinda or Mr. Gatling (or Miss Isobel) marrying. One summer day, however, their continuing threesome was suddenly jeopardized when Mr. Gatling was thrown from his horse and severely injured, the prognosis for his recovery very bleak. Belinda sat at his bedside day after day, night after night. She sang to him, read to him, and prayed for him. She literally refused to let him die and, ultimately, she was victorious in the tug of war that had suspended him between life and death. Mr. Gatling was touched and grateful beyond all words. The words he finally did say to her were the marriage proposal she had hoped for since a schoolgirl. Miss Isobel said that while their union had not started as a love match, their married life was one of mutual devotion and sincere affection – the kind of committed relationship every new bride and groom dream will be theirs.

Among the guests attending the wedding was the widowed Melanie Husted Ward to whom Belinda was like a combination of both little sister and daughter. Having lost her dear husband, she wore mostly black, which made her stand out among the other guests who were dressed more gaily. Mrs. Ward was accompanied by her two daughters and, during the celebratory wedding meal, those three ladies were seated across from Miss Isobel. Belinda had already told Miss Isobel about Mrs. Ward's husband's tragic death knowing that Miss Isobel and her mother Emmeline would be seated near them at the table. Miss Isobel remembered how she tried to make conversation carefully so as to avoid the subject of Mr. Ward's death. That was the first time she met Mrs. Ward but their mutual connection to the newly-married C.C. and Belinda Gatling would bring them into each other's paths multiple times after that.

On one of those occasions, a dual celebration of the Gatlings' tenth wedding anniversary and Belinda's fortieth birthday in 1895, came the fateful incident between Mrs. Ward and Miss Isobel. Mrs. Ward, to whom Belinda was almost "family," was naturally predisposed to being protective of her. Having noticed the closeness of the relationship between Mr. Gatling and Miss Isobel, those protective instincts presented themselves in the form of a suspicion that Miss Isobel had designs on Mr. Gatling. During the party celebrating the birthday and anniversary, Mrs. Ward had apparently decided to be vigilant in observing interactions between Mr. Gatling and Miss Isobel with a mind to confirming her suspicions. Noticing that both of the parties she wished to keep under surveillance were suddenly missing from the parlor, she stepped out into the hall and, hearing voices speaking in hushed tones, followed to the origin of those sounds. Peeking around the corner of the doorway to Mr. Gatling's study, she saw him and Miss Isobel facing each other just inches apart and then saw Miss Isobel lay her hand on Mr. Gatling's shoulder in a tender manner. She cleared her throat to announce her proximity and told Mr. Gatling that she thought he was needed in the parlor. When he left and she was alone in the study with Miss Isobel, she asked (all but demanded) to know what they had been whispering about. When Miss Isobel declined to say, Mrs. Ward turned on her heel to leave saying that she knew very well what Miss Isobel was about and threatening to tell Belinda Gatling "just what was going on."

In fact, nothing of the kind was "going on" but there was a secret known only to Miss Isobel and Mr. Gatling: Belinda, who had not been feeling well off and on for some months, had been diagnosed with cancer. Mr. Gatling had not yet had the strength to tell her what the doctor had confided to him but he had told the grim news to his oldest friend, Miss Isobel. That was what they were huddled together discussing.

Both Mrs. Ward and Miss Isobel stayed the night at the house and, at breakfast the following morning, Mrs. Ward cast a cold stare in Miss Isobel's direction. Belinda was happily talking about how lovely the party had been, thanking her husband (and Miss Isobel) for their help in planning it. Belinda being an avid reader like herself, Miss Isobel had given her a special edition of the complete works of Nathaniel Hawthorne. Beautifully bound in leather and marble boards with gilt lettering on the spine, Belinda was most happy to add it to their library. In thanking Miss Isobel, she reminisced about how, since they were adolescent girls, they had both loved to read and enter into discussions about books. She specifically mentioned that the first Hawthorne story they had read was the one they still liked the best: *The Scarlet Letter*. Miss Isobel responded in agreement, commenting about the strength and resoluteness of the long-suffering Hester Prynne.

Mrs. Ward, no doubt seething as she listened to her dear wronged Belinda lavishly thanking her "best friend" Miss Isobel, broke her icy silence. Directing her words toward Miss Isobel, she asked if Miss Isobel meant to make a "fornicator" into a heroine. Miss Isobel was, for once, without words . . . as was Belinda Gatling. Mr. Gatling stepped in with a chuckle saying that the value of a book, like beauty, is in the eye of the beholder and suggested that the subject of Mistress Prynne's character be tabled in lieu of more pleasant breakfast conversation.

Not surprisingly, Miss Isobel made her departure directly after breakfast was finished but managed to tell Mr. Gatling about her encounter with Mrs. Ward in his study the evening before. When he escorted Mrs. Ward to the steamer that would take her home to Alexandria, he confronted her in a most gentlemanly manner making it perfectly clear that she had drawn a very wrong and very unjust conclusion about Miss Isobel and, by extension, about him.

Whether she believed him or not, she never made good on her threat to speak to Belinda and a merciful thing that was as Belinda was taken not long after by the cancer that Miss Isobel and Mr. Gatling had been discussing that fateful night. Ironically, there was little doubt that had Mrs. Ward made her accusation known to Belinda, the result would have been something quite different than the gratitude Mrs. Ward might have expected. Belinda, knowing the charge for what it was, baseless, would not have turned against her husband and Miss Isobel but may very well have done just that with respect to her old friend Melanie Ward. At the time of Belinda's death, Mrs. Ward was traveling and so was not in Norfolk for the funeral. As such, before their chance meeting at Dr. Steel's lecture in Alexandria, Miss Isobel and Mrs. Melanie Ward had not seen or heard from each other since the "fornicator" incident at the Gatlings' breakfast table more than fifteen years prior.

TEN: "IF ONE CANNOT ENJOY READING A BOOK OVER AND OVER AGAIN, THERE IS NO USE IN READING IT AT ALL."
-OSCAR WILDE

Unbeknownst to me for some time, the chance meeting between Miss Isobel and Mrs. Ward had affected a truce and reconciliation between those two independent and strong-willed ladies. It started I believe with a carefully composed thank you note sent by Miss Isobel to Mrs. Ward after our return to Norfolk. Beyond expressing the conventional gratitude for the hospitality Mrs. Ward had shown us, it contained two short sentences that in my estimation, while not the raising of a white flag per se, had the distinct scent of an olive branch. I wondered if telling me the story of her past history with Mrs. Ward and their rift had made Miss Isobel weigh the cause of their falling out against the significance of the people and events that had brought them together. The tone of the thank you note was warmly set by its opening, "Dear Mellie," but it was the two closing sentences that exposed the writer's true purpose in sending it: "The hand of chance or serendipity brought me unexpectedly to your table. The door separating us was opened; I stepped over the threshold for a visit and found instead a reunion." It was signed simply "Izzy."

The two former friends, once again on good terms, had corresponded frequently using their missives to share news of their activities and interests and to engage in discussions (and likely spirited debates) on a variety of subjects including politics, religion, the arts and, heaven help them, literary tastes. I became aware of their letter-writing only after Mrs. Ward fell ill some six months after we had been to her home for dinner. I had stopped by Miss Isobel's house one afternoon and found her in the parlor examining a small package that had just been delivered. She carefully tore open the outer paper wrapper to reveal a book. A broad smile erupted on her face as she held up the book so that I could read the title: *The Scarlet Letter*. The inside cover of the book bore a handwritten inscription with a familiar name: *Melanie A. Ward, Alexandria, Virginia*. There was a note accompanying the book. When Miss Isobel opened it and began reading the message the smile fell from her face. The note was from Mrs. Ward's daughter. Her mother had been stricken with sudden paralysis and was in a very bad way. No doubt realizing the seriousness of her condition, Mrs. Ward had given her daughters instructions regarding things she wanted done. Among her directives was that her copy of *The Scarlet Letter* should be sent to Miss Isobel with a note to let her friend know what had happened. Melanie A. Ward was seventy-five years old when she passed away in June 1913 at her home on South Washington Street, leaving two married daughters, their husbands, and several grandchildren to mourn her passing. Mr. Gatling and Miss Isobel traveled to Alexandria to attend the funeral of their friend.

Miss Isobel and Mr. Gatling did not return as expected two days after the funeral. When both were absent from a scheduled Library Board meeting without giving notice, inquiries were made at Mr. Gatling's office, the response being that they had remained in Alexandria to handle some "business matters." When I heard that they had extended their stay in Alexandria, I went over to Miss Isobel's home to talk with Katie. I rang the bell but there was no answer. I went away and returned several hours later, rang the bell, and again no one responded to the door. Something was wrong, I felt sure. I talked with Mrs. Boone and she agreed it was unlike Mr. Gatling or Miss Isobel to be so remiss and inconsiderate of others and, further, it was strange that Katie was now also gone without notice or explanation.

Ten days later Miss Isobel, Mr. Gatling, and Katie returned together from Alexandria. Miss Isobel had become faint during Mrs. Ward's funeral and by the following day was extremely weak and unable to travel home. Mrs. Ward's daughters insisted that she and Mr. Gatling stay at their mother's home until Miss Isobel had regained her strength. All assumed that Miss Isobel had been overcome by the stress of the sudden trip to Alexandria and the death of Mrs. Ward. Two days later, when Miss Isobel remained thoroughly drained and unable to leave her bed without help, a doctor was summoned. Katie, not waiting to be called for, arrived at the Ward home just before the doctor. It appeared that Miss

Isobel was once again down with the grippe, perhaps the result of some lingering susceptibility due to her earlier bout with the same ailment. She had a low-grade fever this time along with a nagging cough. She had several restless nights and Katie faithfully sat up with her, changing her perspiration-soaked night clothes as needed. As had happened the last time, the crisis finally passed and Miss Isobel began to regain her strength and appetite. Released from the doctor's care a few days later, she was at last well enough to make the trip home to Norfolk.

Mrs. Boone and I visited Miss Isobel as soon as Katie said she was able to receive us. We came into the parlor to find her wearing a lovely silk dressing gown and sitting in one of the deep blue damask upholstered chairs near the window. I noticed that there was a silver-handled cane propped near the chair, the sight of that causing a twinge in my stomach. Was she still that weak? Her face was a bit paler than usual and she appeared to have a touch of rouge on her cheeks and a bit of color on her lips. We did not stay too long as we did not want to overtire her. On the way out, we attempted to get Katie to give us more information about Miss Isobel's illness and expected recovery to no avail. She told us what we had already heard: it was another bout of the grippe. As we walked home, Mrs. Boone and I said very little to each other, neither wanting to speak of our surprise or concern. I told Mrs. Boone that I was going to go see Mr. Gatling in the hope that he would tell me more. Something was very wrong and I was determined to know the truth of it.

I had an appointment with Mr. Gatling for my quarterly portfolio review three days later. Going to the office always reminded me of Andrew Pritchard even though a new face, that of a middle-aged bookkeeper, now occupied his desk. Usually I would then wonder how long it would be before stepping over that threshold would no longer trigger thoughts of Andrew Pritchard . . . . but not this time. I was focused only on getting the truth about Miss Isobel's condition.

I listened patiently as Mr. Gatling went through the portfolio of investments and updated me on my financial position. He mentioned that it had been nearly a year since I made the decision to delay (or forego) continuing my education and asked if I had any plans in mind in that regard. I was distracted and he had to ask the question twice to get my attention. I told him that I was still unsure about whether college or business would be right for me and so would likely wait until early the following year to make a decision. As he began gathering up papers and replacing them in a large folder with my name on the flap, I cleared my throat. He looked up and I believe he read the expression on my face. Before I could say anything, he reminded me that Miss Isobel was a strong and determined woman . . . and one who valued her independence and privacy. She was loathe to ask for help despite her delight in helping others. His words sent a shiver through me, not for what they said but for what I was sure they meant. I reminded Mr. Gatling that Miss Isobel was my legal guardian making us "like family." I pressed on saying that I had already lost all the blood family I ever had and was both "entitled" and strong enough to be told the truth.   Mr. Gatling appeared a bit taken back by my forwardness but I could tell he was not affronted as he, more than most anyone, understood my attachment to Miss Isobel. He looked at me sympathetically and said he would speak to Miss Isobel about my concerns and encourage her to talk candidly with me about her illness.

I would like to say I waited *patiently* but, in truth, I waited anxiously, *very* anxiously.   As my mind called up all kinds of dire possibilities, I told myself that the truth could hardly be as bad as my imaginings. In fact, the truth would fall much closer to those fearful thoughts than I had honestly expected.   Mrs. Boone and I were asked to come by to visit Miss Isobel about a week after I had pressed Mr. Gatling to tell me what was wrong.   We sat silent as Miss Isobel confided that she had been diagnosed with consumption. Both bouts of what appeared to be the grippe were actually the beginnings of an active case of tuberculosis. She was very matter-of-fact in talking about her illness, fully in control of both her demeanor and the conversation.

Mrs. Boone was clearly shaken but did her best to keep her composure and, as always, asked if she could "please" be of service to Miss Isobel and Katie in some way. As for me, I felt as if kicked in the gut but, taking my lead from Miss Isobel and owing to my own reluctance to display my emotions to others, I leaned forward, took her hand and simply said that I was "sure" everything would be all right. That night, in the privacy of my own bed, a storm of tears ran down my face. I knew enough about consumption to know that it was too often a deadly disease, a scourge that had defied medical cures for decades. Once taking hold in the lungs of its victims, it stole their breath and then their lives.

It was no surprise to find out that Mr. Gatling had engaged multiple medical specialists to examine Miss Isobel, confirm the diagnosis of tuberculosis, and recommend courses of medication and other treatments. There were things that could be done but nothing that contradicted the diagnosis or promised a cure. I spent hours researching at the Library, intent on learning everything I could about the disease including the typical course of the illness and the history of efforts to discover effective treatment or a cure.

As expected, Miss Isobel thanked Mrs. Boone and me for our offers of help but said they were "unnecessary." Just the same, we took to visiting more frequently, not waiting for an invitation or even asking before arriving at the door. Miss Isobel looked sometimes mildly annoyed at us dropping in but kept her feelings to herself and we could see that our presence, if nothing else, gave relief to Katie. Mr. Gatling was also often at the house and was quite devoted to Miss Isobel.

As the weeks went by, I found myself losing interest in my work at the Library. Miss Isobel had good days but could not be said to be "recovering." She ate decently (Katie made whatever she wanted) but was losing weight. Her bouts of coughing, still sporadic, racked her small frame. Mr. Gatling had been talking to her about "taking the fresh air" in the country, a much-recommended treatment for consumption. I resolved that if she agreed to go, I would be going with her. Not easily convinced, she put off any decision on traveling to the country. It was a hot, humid summer in Norfolk and the thought of leaving the city for the no-doubt cooler climes of the country sounded most appealing to me. In the intervening weeks, Miss Isobel rarely went out and Mrs. Boone and I were with her on an almost daily basis, keeping her company and helping Katie. Courses of medications and treatments started and finished with, at best, seeming to slow progression of Miss Isobel's symptoms. Katie held herself together, almost stoic in her dedication to keeping routines and ensuring that doctors' orders were followed to the letter. More than once, late at night when I stayed over at the house, I heard her crying softly in the bedroom adjoining where I slept. I wanted to console her but I suspected that it was important that I did not inadvertently rob her of her veneer of strength and implacability.

"Small talk" was not easy as the days went by. There was only so much local news (and gossip) to talk about and precious little distraction was derived from that when all our thoughts were preoccupied with Miss Isobel's condition. One day as my mind wandered, I thought about the dinner at Mrs. Ward's house in Alexandria. It seemed so long ago yet it was only about eight months before, a time when both Mrs. Ward and Miss Isobel were well and lively and feeling their way through a chance meeting that neither expected would rekindle their personal connection. I recalled Miss Isobel's obvious amusement when she unwrapped Mrs. Ward's gift of her own copy of *The Scarlet Letter*, a clever and symbolic proof of their restored friendship, only to find out that it was in essence a bequest from a dying Mrs. Ward. I felt ashamed that the copy of *The Scarlet Letter* gifted to me by Miss Isobel continued to sit unopened and ignored on a table in my bedroom. From that came an idea that I thought would fill the evening hours with Miss Isobel while also solving the problem of my unread copy of *The Scarlet Letter*. I confessed to Miss Isobel that I had been struggling in my attempts to read the book she had given me and suggested that it might help if I read it aloud to her and had the benefit of her familiarity with the text, its themes and the author's intent in telling the story. She smiled warmly and said it was a "very sensible idea."

I did not have my copy of the book with me; it was, as usual, languishing on my bedside table at home. I asked Miss Isobel where in her bookshelves I would find her copy. She directed me to the right shelf and I noticed two copies of the book, both in brown cloth covers and looking, but for the amount of wear, identical. I lifted one out and opened it finding an inscription indicating that the book had originally been given (in 1854) from one brother to another as a gift on the occasion of his thirteenth birthday. Miss Isobel, leaning on her cane, came alongside me as I was examining the inscription. She reached out, gently took the book from my hands and replaced it on the shelf. She drew out the other copy, opened it to Mrs. Ward's inscription, handed it to me without a word and resumed her seat. I took her deliberateness in switching one book for the other as signaling that her recently lost friend was still much on her mind. I imagined that she would derive comfort from seeing me turn the pages of that old book as I read from it, knowing it was a gift that symbolized her reconciliation with Mrs. Ward. How many times do you hear people lament what they "could have" or "should have" done . . . if only they knew that the sands of the hourglass that measured their opportunity to do so were all but gone? In her sorrow at Mrs. Ward's passing, Miss Isobel must know that she had quite literally, by her own hand and pen, bested the hourglass measuring Mrs. Ward's remaining time on this earth.

As the hot summer days of August waned, September began, and the transition to autumn followed, I often read aloud a few pages of Mrs. Ward's book in the evening before Miss Isobel retired and we did discuss those readings, that being a great help to my understanding and appreciation of Hawthorne's story of the power of love, hate, revenge, and redemption. I soon began to look forward to those readings and conversations for my own benefit and because I could see a spark light her eyes once again when she talked about the resoluteness of Hester Prynne, comparing that to the fatal frailties of the two men whose secrets she kept despite both being utterly unworthy of her sacrifice.

With the weather becoming more moderate, Mr. Gatling had resumed his urging that Miss Isobel "take the fresh air" in the country as so many of those afflicted with tuberculosis were advised to do. I told her that I had taken a leave from my job at the Library in anticipation of accompanying her and by way of coaxing, joked that I would be bringing *The Scarlet Letter* with us. Katie and Mrs. Boone in their turns joined the chorus in entreating Miss Isobel to go and offering to join her for the excursion. I have no doubt that Miss Isobel was fully aware that her condition was not really improving and had made her own inquiries about treatment avenues. In any event, she finally agreed to hear Mr. Gatling out about traveling to the Catawba Valley for a month-long respite at the Roanoke Red Sulphur Springs Resort near Salem, Virginia. The resort was a well-known mountain "escape" for those seeking clean air, healthy food, peace, and quiet. Water from the mineral springs was said to be effective in treatment of diseases of the lungs and was known as "Catawba Iron All Healing" water. Many of the visitors coming to the resort were, in fact, tuberculosis sufferers and the facilities had been expanding to serve as a sanatorium offering a regimen focused on combating that disease. The property was more than five hundred acres offering specialized exercise programs, miles of walking trails, landscaped gardens, pavilions, and "cure" cottages for guests.

All of us traveled out to Catawba with Miss Isobel, she referring to us as her "entourage." Katie and I remained at Catawba with her while Mr. Gatling and Mrs. Boone stayed just a couple days to see us properly settled and then headed home to Norfolk. Our cottage was a bit more "rustic" than Miss Isobel was accustomed to, a small and basic wood structure. I saw her eyebrows raise as we were shown to the cottage but she made no complaint. While the cottage was spare, the immediate grounds and the scenic beauty of the surrounding mountain vistas were quite the opposite, rich and breath-taking. And, as promised, the air was fresh and there was an overall atmosphere of natural serenity. We began taking short walks with Miss Isobel taking care not to overtire her. We would sometimes sit under the gazebo that sheltered a marble fountain that dispensed some of that famed Catawba healing water. A taste of that notable curative convinced us that it must be a "tonic" as it had a mildly unpleasant odor and a distinct aftertaste like some of the medicines our mothers had administered to us saying they were "good for you."   Unlike Catawba's signature "beverage," the food was quite tasty and undeniably fresh, much of it locally grown or made fresh daily at the resort.

I continued to read to Miss Isobel in the evenings and, as much as she was able, we participated in the offered exercise programs and other activities. Each week, even each day I must confess, I looked for signs that she was getting stronger or coughing less. Looking back now, I must admit that any positive change I saw was more a wish on my part than fact. As the planned month-long stay neared its end, I thanked God not for curing her but for the gift of time spent with her in such close companionship. I did not express my disappointment to Katie as I felt fully sure that she was of the same mind. Over those four weeks, neither of us approached the other to talk about Miss

Isobel's "recovery" progress . . . because we saw no change and to talk would mean the necessity of acknowledging that to each other. It never occurred to me then that Miss Isobel herself had not spoken about the good the country air and exercise were doing her. Like Hester Prynne, the woman whose story she so loved, she remained resolute and, no doubt wanting to spare our feelings, carried her burden in silence.

Just days before our scheduled return to Norfolk, as I headed to the laundry to retrieve our finished wash, I encountered a man pushing a wheelchair in front of me on the path. As I approached from behind in something of a hurry as I had almost forgotten we had laundry to be picked up, I politely said "excuse me" as I stepped off the path to go around them. The man turned his head in my direction and my eyes met those of Andrew Pritchard. Time stood still as each of us recovered from the shock of seeing the other. Before I could speak, Andrew leaned down to the young woman in the wheelchair and introduced me to his wife, Ophelia. Ophelia was painfully thin, her delicate face gaunt with the effects of illness. I could see the effort it took for her to raise a smile and nod her head in response. I walked around to face her and returned the smile saying that I had met Andrew briefly during his apprenticeship in Norfolk and was "most pleased" to make her acquaintance. Looking apprehensive, Andrew asked what had brought me to Catawba, his voice trailing off as he said "not illness I hope." I explained that I had come with my guardian Isobel Verity, a close friend of Mr. Gatling, she being ill with consumption. Anxious to remove myself from a situation that was awkward on multiple levels, I told Andrew that we were preparing to leave for Norfolk and I must get back to Miss Isobel and packing for the trip home. I returned my eyes to Ophelia's and, not knowing what to say, bent down and wished her "good day," a farewell I now remember sadly as a foolish platitude delivered to a person whose days must have been miserable.

ELEVEN: "NAME ME NO NAMES FOR MY DISEASE, I TELL YOU I AM NONE OF THESE." ~WITTER BYNNER

Being back in Norfolk after a month in the country made me notice the swirling sounds, city smells, and bustling activity that replaced the natural songs, sweet scents, and placid pace of Catawba. I had to admit that, despite my disappointment at Miss Isobel not having achieved a "cure" there, our time at Catawba was physically restful and mentally restorative. Just the same, I was glad to be home again and Miss Isobel was clearly pleased to feel the succor that comes of returning to one's own nest.

Once home, she became somewhat self-absorbed in activities that she did not share with us such as what appeared to be the writing of letters that were not posted. I arrived one afternoon (unannounced) to find her solicitor, Mr. Treadway, putting on his coat and preparing to leave the house. There were some things even I, with my chronic excuse of uncontrollable curiosity, could not ask and so I was left to wonder about the purpose of his visit. Looking back, I can hardly believe I was so naïve as not to have suspected why he was summoned. I should have recognized Miss Isobel's movements for what they were: the tidying up of her life in response to a reckoning with the specter of death. I could not see it then as I believed her stronger than her disease and so was unable, unwilling, or lacking the inner strength to accept the changes my own eyes were seeing.

One evening after reading from *The Scarlet Letter* at her bedside, I looked up to see her dozing off. I closed the book and stood, placing it on the stand next to her bed. Before turning down the lamp and leaving I smoothed the quilt covering her and bent down and kissed her forehead. Her skin was warm, too warm, and clammy and when my head was near hers I clearly heard her congested breath sounds and the low persistent wheezing coming from her chest. Taking one more look before leaving the room, the image of Ophelia Pritchard's pale face came suddenly to my mind and, for the first time, palpable fear washed over me. I felt heat rising through me and a blackness coming in like a veil over my eyes. I tried to steady myself by leaning on the chair I had been sitting on minutes earlier. My last recollection was doing that and then taking a few steps in the direction of the hallway.

I hadn't gotten very far. When I came to myself, I was on my back straddled under the open doorway, how I got there unknown to me. Within seconds Katie came to my side having heard "a noise" above her and thinking perhaps Miss Isobel had fallen. Miss Isobel was still sound asleep, thankfully. The plush pile of the lovely blue and red patterned William Morris hallway runner had apparently afforded some cushioning for my descent to the ground. Katie ordered me to stay as I was while she examined me for any obvious signs of serious injury and, seeing none, helped me up. Upon rising I felt some discomfort in my shoulder but not enough to signal a break or fracture I was sure. Katie helped me to the bedroom where I often spent the night, helped me undress, and then returned with a pot of tea and a plaster for my shoulder. She let out a small gasp when she came into the room. In the short time she had been gone, I had sprouted quite a nasty red bump on my forehead. She turned tail and left, soon coming back with ice for that swelling. By the next morning I was stiff and bruised and I walked like the Tin Man in Mr. Baum's children's book *The Wonderful Wizard of Oz*. Looking in the mirror to get the full effect of the now purplish-blue egg on my forehead, I remembered reading that book to the children in the Library reading program several years past. It seemed so long ago now.

I did not tell Katie what preceded (or perhaps precipitated) the fall and said that when I was trying to quietly exit the room, walking backwards and pulling the door closed, I must have tripped on the edge of the carpet runner. There was no need to worry her or Miss Isobel by recounting the sudden loss of composure that had effectively dispatched my knees out from under me and delivered me to the floor. Miss Isobel's eyes went wide when she saw the wounded warrior that met her at breakfast. The story of my clumsiness was recounted and Miss Isobel commented that I had been most considerate in falling on the carpet and not crying out causing her to wake. She suggested some herbs for a poultice that should be applied liberally to my forehead for the next few days to promote more rapid healing. Absent a successful result with that, she predicted that I would see a rainbow of colors - blue, purple, green and yellow – when I looked in the mirror over the next two weeks. We all laughed at that but, as was too often the case with Miss Isobel's illness, that laughing loosed a wave of coughing that shook her small frame mercilessly.

When I returned home later that day, I did tell Mrs. Boone what really happened to me the night before. I adored and looked up to Miss Isobel but it was Mrs. Boone who was in many ways a surrogate mother to me. I found it easy to tell her my feelings, my thoughts, and even my concerns. I cannot say that she ever tried to insinuate herself into the role of my "mother" or act in general as a parent to me but no one, after the loss of my own parents, was closer to being that for me than she. Perhaps it was because Mrs. Boone was an open book while Miss Isobel, for all her kindness and generosity, was a book that would be opened only when and so far as she would permit. Knowing Mrs. Boone came with the full knowledge of the life-defining tragedies that had befallen her thus providing a key to understanding her as a person. As much as I had learned about Miss Isobel, I could not shake off the feeling that there was much more murky water in that well.

Mrs. Boone had me continue the herbal poultice and also made a salve for my shoulder which, truth be told, ached like the very devil and was also sporting a colorful bruise. Mrs. Boone said I should consider seeing the doctor and I said I would do so if the aching in my shoulder changed to actual pain or movement of my arm became restricted in any way. Fortunately that did not become the case and it was just a matter of the slow healing of deep and very tender bruising.

My "convalescence" kept me home for a few days, partly from vanity about my discolored forehead and partly due to the rather pungent odor of the salve and poultice. When I next visited Miss Isobel, Mrs. Boone came with me and brought a small kettle of her most delicious homemade chicken soup. When we rang, the door was opened by Mr. Gatling, who did not smile and in whose face the signs of strain were unmistakable. He motioned us inside and began to speak in low tones telling us that Miss Isobel had a very difficult night and was most weak. He said she was refusing to eat and that when he coaxed her to take a few spoons of grits she did so only to launch into a terrible fit of coughing, some of it bringing up phlegm tinged with blood. He said Katie was sitting with Miss Isobel helping her with the reading of the mail as she did each day.

We asked if we might please stay despite Miss Isobel being so poorly, promising not to tax her or even go to see her unless he and Katie agreed we could do so. He touched my cheek and told us he was most grateful to have us there. Mrs. Boone brought the soup kettle to the kitchen and warmed up a small amount of just the broth. When Katie came down, Mrs. Boone suggested trying to see if Miss Isobel could sip some of the broth from a drinking glass or tea cup as the chicken stock would provide at least some needed nutrition for her. If she were able to tolerate it, then later she could have more of the broth with some finely shredded chicken and vegetables which would be more fortifying. This plan was set into motion and was reasonably successful in getting some small portions of soup into Miss Isobel. The doctor had been called, even though, at this stage, there was little he might do but to assist in making Miss Isobel more "comfortable."

Mr. Gatling sat vigil at her bedside that night, alternately moistening her cracked lips with a soft white cloth dipped in cool water and then delicately wiping the small beads of perspiration from her brow. His touch was one fit for the handling of a fragile porcelain doll, so very tender that it raised tears in my eyes. He would not accept relief from any of us but was happy to have us there with him and near her. As he once again took a dry cloth to her brow, he carefully lifted the hair that lay across it and I saw what appeared to be a faded scar near the hairline. Miss Isobel had always worn a sort of wavy side-swept lock of hair across that part of her forehead so I had never before seen that mark. It was about an inch and a half long and somewhat irregular in shape as if it had healed without medical attention or any stitching to close it. I immediately recognized it from the story Miss Isobel had shared with me after giving me Frederick Bentell's copy of *The Scarlet Letter* and I hoped to still have the chance to ask how she came to have that life-long reminder of her earliest days.

We hoped that Miss Isobel would once again weather the crisis and rally, the morning bringing signs of the worst having passed. The new day brought no improvement this time. She grew quieter, less delirious than she had been at times the night before. Mr. Gatling spoke to her in hushed tones, only some of which I could make out. I did hear him call her "dearest Izzy" as he told her that his "beloved Lindy" would soon greet her with "the warmest of hugs and tender kisses." Katie, who came and went all night as she cared for Miss Isobel and for us, quietly joined us at Miss Isobel's bedside. Just a quarter hour later, Miss Isobel's lids lifted for the first time that morning and she extended her two bone-thin arms a few inches above the quilt that was covering her. She spoke but one word: "Mama" and with that was gone from us. I could not stay in the room as the sight of the tears running down Mr. Gatling's rugged face as he held Miss Isobel's limp hand to his cheek cut me to the quick. He was devastated . . . inconsolable and vulnerable in the same way my own father had been when death took my mother from him. Katie and Mrs. Boone soon followed me out of the room leaving Mr. Gatling alone to say his final farewell to Miss Isobel in privacy and allowing him a chance to regain his equilibrium before seeing us again.

The three of us sat silent around the kitchen table still somewhat in disbelief, miles removed from each other, lost in our own thoughts. That silence was only broken when Mr. Gatling entered the kitchen. He went to the sink and splashed some water on his face and then turned back to us. He had regained his composure for the most part, although still visibly shaken. He discussed what must be done including the funeral arrangements and the carrying out of instructions left by Miss Isobel in anticipation of this day. He said he would contact the funeral director and Miss Isobel's solicitor immediately and then would stop home to "clean up" and put on fresh clothes. He went to Miss Isobel's library table and took out a lovely antique burl travel desk. He lifted the lid on a small black lacquer casket that sat on a nearby shelf and retrieved a key that unlocked the travel desk. The little portable desk held a half-dozen or more sealed envelopes each labeled in Miss Isobel's hand. He opened one of the envelopes, unfolded the single page inside it and scanned the content. He then handed the sheet of paper to me and asked that I arrange to contact each of the persons listed on the page notifying them of Miss Isobel's death. I nodded indicating that I would and, looking at the list, I immediately saw the names of Melanie Ward's two daughters among others.

The list of about two dozen names had all the familiar marks of its author. Organized, clearly delineated down to the smallest detail, and presented in her graceful flowing hand. Beyond the names and addresses of the people to be contacted, each entry also instructed the manner of communication (whether by telegram or postal letter for instance) to be used in delivering the sad news. One of those to be notified was Mr. Sargeant, the head of the Library. I thought it best to go to the Library, tell Mr. Sargeant first and then quietly gather the staff to tell them as well. I knew that either Mr. Sargeant or Mr. Gatling would contact the Library Board members so there was no need for me to do so. The news of Miss Isobel's death was received with much sincere sadness throughout the halls and rooms of the Library. It was much the same around the city as Miss Isobel was known for her community involvement and philanthropy. The day after her death the *Landmark*, Norfolk's most popular newspaper, ran a beautifully written memorial piece about Miss Isobel and her contributions in promoting literacy in the greater Norfolk community.

Mrs. Boone and I stayed at Miss Isobel's home during the days leading up to her funeral. We wanted to be with Katie and all three of us being in the house made it easier for Mr. Gatling who, with Mr. Treadway's help, had taken charge of the execution of Miss Isobel's final requests and the settlement of her estate. Among the instructions Miss Isobel left was that there was to be no viewing of her body at her home or elsewhere. She requested that mourners gather at the cemetery and that there be a short service at her gravesite before burial. Mr. Gatling made sure her wishes were honored in that and every other regard.

The afternoon before the funeral, the Library Board had met and voted to close the Library for the funeral in respect of Miss Isobel's dedication to that institution . . . and to allow the staff the opportunity to attend the funeral. I had stopped in at the Library to confirm that Mr. Sargeant would say a few words during the interment service at the cemetery and was there when the announcement was made that the Library would be closed the following day for the funeral. I stayed a while longer and availing myself of art materials I knew were stored in the supplies closet, I made a carefully lettered placard stating that the Library was closed for Miss Isobel's funeral. My thoughts traveled back to the day I approached Mrs. Watts of the Norfolk Ladies Club to ask if I might help with their preparations for the Jamestown Exposition. I visualized the words "Jamestown Exposition" that I had so carefully lettered, convincing Mrs. Watts to accept my help. I put the art supplies back in the closet and pulled out the folding easel stand. On my way out, as the Library was closing for the day, I carried the easel stand through the foyer and out the front doors, unfolded its legs and put the closing announcement in place.

On an unseasonably mild November day, an elegant horse-drawn hearse carried Miss Isobel's casket slowly through the streets of Norfolk. The large grey horses held their heads high as they marched toward the cemetery. Mrs. Boone, Katie, Mr. Gatling, and I walked behind the hearse arm-in-arm and as we progressed through town others, both mourners and residents, fell in after us. Others stopped on the sidewalk, women nodding and men removing their hats in respect. The service at the gravesite was not long but included touching tributes from Mr. Sargeant, Mr. Gatling, and others along with prayers led by Miss Isobel's minister. Miss Isobel had instructed that an after-funeral repast be held at her home, a simple buffet where mourners would gather casually, serving themselves and free to stay or go as they saw fit thereafter. The repast went very much as she had intended. Those who wanted to come did so. Those who wanted to eat did, others just came to express their sympathy or share memories. The warm informality was comforting and allowed us to spend time with those who came. I recognized most of the people in attendance at the funeral with the exception of an elderly man who stood apart from the gathered mourners at the cemetery and appeared to be observing the services from a distance. I thought I would approach him should he come to the repast but he did not and I reasoned that he had been at the cemetery to visit someone's grave and, seeing us, had stopped for a few moments out of curiosity. That conclusion would later be proven wrong.

Part Three: Belle

"I have laughed, in bitterness and agony of heart, at the contrast between what I seem and what I am!"

~Nathaniel Hawthorne (*The Scarlet Letter*)

TWELVE: "ALL WARS ARE CIVIL WARS, BECAUSE ALL MEN ARE BROTHERS."
- FRANÇOIS FENELON

The value of Miss Isobel's estate was even more significant than I had imagined. While I did not see an actual accounting of course, the generous bequests amounted to what in my estimation was a great deal of money. I assisted Mr. Gatling and Mr. Treadway when asked and was grateful to be some small part of carrying out Miss Isobel's final wishes. Taking care of the estate kept Mr. Gatling very busy and I thought that a good diversion from his grief.

I stayed at Miss Isobel's house with Katie and helped her do a necessary inventory of Miss Isobel's possessions. Although Miss Isobel was never extravagant and, in my experience, had little interest in material things, her home exhibited her unique and tasteful style. Rather than the fine antiques or elegant furnishings that I believed she could have afforded, her weakness was for one-of-a-kind, handcrafted items that were the work of local artists, aspiring sculptors, potters, and artisans working in metal or materials such as leather or wood. She once told me that while she could walk right past a jeweler's store window, she felt compelled to visit every booth at a craft fair or open air market whether in Norfolk or somewhere else she might be. Her home showcased the treasures she discovered on those outings. Among her bequests were amounts to be given to some of her favorite local artisans to encourage their continued work.

The range of bequests included one to the local Negro Literacy League for the purchase of books to be distributed to Negro children. The League had been lobbying for a branch library for the use of Negro residents and there was increasing talk that a small space would be allocated in a local school building for that purpose. Miss Isobel intended to make sure that, branch library or not, books would be available to Negro children. She also endowed scholarships at both white and "colored" high schools for graduates to continue their education with the goal of becoming teachers in the Norfolk public schools.

Miss Isobel left Katie a generous sum representing a single pension payment. In that fashion, Katie could decide how and when to use those funds rather than receiving periodic payments over the remainder of her life. Even Mrs. Boone received a small sum much to her sincere surprise, no doubt a gesture to ensure that she knew Miss Isobel counted her a friend. Mr. Gatling did not mention any bequest to me and, while I thought that strange, I did not ask. I had imagined Miss Isobel would want me to have some small personal memento of her, perhaps another of her antiquarian books selected especially for me or the delicate carved bone brooch that she wore so often. I flushed at my feeling of being "entitled" to something from her considering all she had done for me already.

Katie and I continued to work on the inventory and were into our second afternoon cataloging Miss Isobel's books, no small undertaking. While most of them would be donated to public and school libraries in the area, some of the rarer antiquarian books were specifically mentioned in Miss Isobel's bequests and were destined for institutions including the Smithsonian, the Virginia Historical Society, and even George Washington's home, Mount Vernon. As we systematically pulled books from one shelf and then the next, I came upon the two early "twin" copies of *The Scarlet Letter,* one the gift of Mrs. Melanie Ward and the other one I had briefly opened months before only to have Miss Isobel return it to the shelf in favor of Mrs. Ward's copy. I look down at the list of specific book bequests and saw that Mrs. Ward's copy was to be returned to her daughters so it could be kept in their family. I did not know if there was a specific instruction as to what was to be done with the other copy. I put Mrs. Ward's book aside and inserted a slip of paper with her address inside the front cover and, turning back to the shelf, withdrew the other copy, opened it and looked for the inscription I remembered seeing on the front endpaper. I read it aloud: "Owen E. Sterling, from his brother Jessup H. Sterling on his 13th birthday, 1854."

My utterance was immediately followed by the sound of books falling to the floor and I turned to see Katie quickly stooping to pick up what she had obviously dropped. Placing the books on a table she asked if she might look at the book I was holding, the Sterling-inscribed copy of *The Scarlet Letter*. I handed it to her and watched her as she gazed down at the open book and lightly passed her index finger over the words of the inscription as if discovering some long lost or secret message. She returned the book to me and simply said that we should "put it aside for now." I nodded my agreement and placed it alongside the books to be distributed as specific bequests of Miss Isobel.

We ended our work as the time was nearing for our evening meal. I thought it best not to ask about the Sterling book thus giving Katie time to bring it up herself. Nothing was said about it over supper and I wondered if she would speak of it. As we cleared the table she finally said, with an air more serious than her usual, that she must talk with me about the book she had asked me to set aside earlier in the day. And so it was that we spent that long winter evening absorbed in the story of the Sterling family of Mississippi.

Taking a deep breath as if to muster her thoughts or perhaps decide where to start, Katie began by asking if I remembered Miss Isobel talking about her mother Emmeline's time as a teacher at Saint Mary's Hall. I said I most certainly did. She reminded me about the student named Amanda who had fallen ill with cholera during the school's summer session and her sister Hattie who had stayed with Emmeline during Amanda's illness. I assured her that I did recall that as well and remembered Miss Isobel saying that

Hattie had developed a personal attachment to Emmeline and corresponded with her over the ensuing years. With that flag planted to mark the prologue to the tale, the first of many revelations followed: Amanda and Hattie's family name was Sterling, they being the sisters of the Jessup Sterling and Owen Sterling recorded in the inscription in that old copy of *The Scarlet Letter*.

Not long after Emmeline and her new daughter arrived back in Norfolk in the late spring of 1865, Emmeline received a small package from her cousin Frederick Bentell in New Orleans. It contained a letter from him and his mother Sarah along with a few other pieces of mail addressed to Emmeline that had arrived in New Orleans just after she had departed for Virginia. Emmeline and young Isobel had been settling into Emmeline's family home, unpacking their small amount of belongings and putting to rights what was still there from the days of her prior residency in that house. Emmeline had learned from her father to put something aside for the inevitable "rainy day" and although she had contributed financially to the Bentell household while living with them, she had left some funds on deposit in a bank account she had opened in Philadelphia during her days working as a teacher at Saint Mary's. Before leaving New Orleans she had posted a letter to the Philadelphia Bentells who had been instrumental in her getting that position letting them know she was expecting to return to Virginia and might need their assistance to make a withdrawal from that account. Among the letters forwarded from New

Orleans was one from the Philadelphia Bentells acknowledging receipt of her letter and offering whatever help she might need to access those funds and have the money sent to her by post or wire as per her instructions.

The package also held two other letters, one from the caretaker confirming that the house was nearly ready for her return and another, postmarked in Mississippi and bearing a familiar handwriting, that of Hattie Sterling. Emmeline hesitated before opening Hattie's letter. So much tragedy had befallen the Sterling family since the start of the war. She said a short prayer before unfolding the pages hoping that Hattie's letter was not sent to share more sad news. While the news could not be categorized as "good," it was not about more death in the Sterling family. Hattie, knowing that Emmeline had roots in Norfolk, and hoping her connections there remained intact, was writing to ask for help for her youngest brother Edward Sterling, a young Confederate soldier. Edward had enlisted in the 18th Mississippi Regiment at the age of fifteen and was later reassigned to the Signal Corps under Major General William Henry Fitzhugh Lee, son of General Robert E. Lee, his unit deployed in Virginia. As she read the beginning portion of the letter, Emmeline feared that Edward had been wounded or fallen ill and was in need of sanctuary. Reading further she saw that although he had been ill months earlier with a bout of scurvy, he had returned to his unit and the support of what would be Robert E. Lee's last campaign. In a battle near Petersburg, Edward had been captured by Union forces and transported to the Point Lookout prisoner of war camp in Maryland where he remained since then. Edward had written to his sisters saying there was talk that, with the surrender at Appomattox, prisoners would be offered release in exchange for agreeing to take an oath of loyalty to the United States of America. He said his health was "passable" considering the scarcity of food, constant wet or damp conditions, non-existent sanitary measures, and severe crowding at the camp. Hattie and her sister Amanda were most anxious to try and get some money to Edward upon his release so that he might arrange transportation to Mississippi after availing himself of some nutritious meals and buying clean clothes for that trip. Hattie was hoping that through Emmeline's connections in Virginia, someone could be found to rendezvous with Edward, bringing him money and helping him prepare for his journey home. Their trepidation and protectiveness needed no explanation considering the toll the war had already taken on the Sterling siblings.

Emmeline attempted to send a telegram to Hattie to tell her that she was in Norfolk and would herself find a way to help Edward but the telegraph lines, although working most of the time, were only for military use – no exceptions. She posted a letter instead and wrote that she would advance any funds needed for Edward's care and transportation. With that done, she set about making plans and eliciting help, her first stop a visit to the home of her old friend, Augustus Gatling. Having heard upon her return that Augustus had married and had a young son, she had already intended to call on them to let Augustus know she was back and to meet his wife and child. Edward Sterling's situation would now give that social call a second and more urgent purpose.

Emmeline lost no time in arranging to call on the Gatlings who received her warmly. Augustus introduced his wife Felicity and his son Cassius, a bright-eyed boy of about ten years old. Felicity was born and raised in Connecticut and had met Augustus when both attended a wedding in Baltimore. The long-distance courtship that followed was vexing to both of them and they resolved to marry about six months later and made their home in Norfolk where Augustus was becoming established as an accountant. By all signs, they appeared a very happy couple . . . a very happy family in fact.

When Felicity excused herself to go and check that Cassius was getting ready for bed as instructed, Emmeline told Augustus about Edward Sterling and her desire to intercept him if and when he should be released from Point Lookout. Her plan was to bring him to her home for a respite before he traveled back to Mississippi. Augustus said that it was Felicity's connections that would be most useful in that regard as she had an uncle who was a major in the Union Army and was stationed in Richmond at the moment. Augustus suggested that he speak with Felicity privately on the subject of assisting Edward Sterling and then apprise Emmeline as to his wife's willingness to help. Emmeline, understanding the magnitude of the favor she was requesting, particularly since she had only just met Felicity, said she would be most grateful if he did so. When Felicity returned to the parlor, Emmeline rose, thanked them both for their hospitality, and said she hoped to return it very soon.

Before she could do that she heard from Augustus. Felicity, touched by the story of such a young soldier who had been through so much, had agreed to help and would contact her uncle as soon as possible to enlist his intercession. Weeks later Felicity's uncle notified her that Edward Sterling was among the next group of prisoners scheduled for release and arrangements had been made for him to be transferred by steamer to the local military authorities at Newport News. Emmeline sent off another letter to Hattie Sterling to tell her the good news.

Edward's release and transport to Newport News came in mid-summer, 1865. In asking for their help, Emmeline had explained to Augustus and Felicity Gatling that Edward Sterling's sisters had been her students at Saint Mary's Hall. During the coach ride to Newport News, Emmeline shared the full story of the three Sterling brothers who had all enlisted in the Confederate Army after the outbreak of the war. The Sterling family had roots first in Tennessee and then in Mississippi where the six Sterling siblings, three boys and three girls, had lived with their parents. They lost their mother to death after childbirth when all six were under twelve years of age and that tragedy was followed not long after by the death of the youngest child, a girl, leaving Edward Sterling the youngest of the five surviving Sterling children. Their father soon turned over the care of his children to his deceased wife's

Hamilton family in Mississippi and thereafter had little role in their upbringing. The Sterling children were loved and well-cared for by their Hamilton relations. Edward's older brothers, Jessup and Owen Sterling, attended the University of Mississippi and, just prior to the start of the war, Jessup had graduated and was preparing for a career as a lawyer. Owen was a student at the University when the war commenced. Both brothers enlisted in a Mississippi Confederate regiment in the early weeks of the war. Edward, being only fourteen years old at the time, did not immediately follow his brothers into the army; his enlistment would come a year later at the tender age of just fifteen.

The Sterling brothers were most proud of their family connection to the revered Confederate, General Malcolm Sterling, and both Jessup and Owen were intent on earning an officer's commission, an objective each of those two young men achieved by the second year of the war. Owen was made a sergeant-major in his Mississippi regiment and was later promoted to lieutenant and adjutant. Jessup realized his most ardent desire when he was detached from his Mississippi unit, commissioned a captain, and reassigned to a unit under none other than his distant cousin General Malcolm Sterling. Battlefield tragedy stalked Jessup, Owen, and General Sterling between the summers of 1862 and 1864, all three being fatally wounded: Jessup at Manassas, Owen near Fredericksburg, and General Sterling near Richmond, the two brothers not yet twenty-five and the General all of thirty.

This last statement by Emmeline was met with an audible gasp from Felicity Gatling who lowered her head at the knowledge of young lives so brutally ended. Sadder still was the truth that there were thousands more men, young and old, lost in a violent struggle that never should have happened.

The coach stopped in front of the building where Felicity's uncle had indicated Edward would be detained until their arrival. Felicity, Emmeline, and Augustus stepped out of the coach, climbed the steep steps to the double doors and entered. Felicity announced herself to the officer at the reception desk handing over a document from her uncle regarding Edward Sterling's release. It seemed so long until a door in the rear of the room opened and a boy was ushered in, his cheeks sunken and his uniform hanging on his slight frame as if he had borrowed it from someone a good deal larger than he. He carried a small well-worn knapsack that he held tightly in his arms and his eyes spoke of concern and suspicion as he took a measure of the strangers awaiting him. This was eighteen-year-old Edward Sterling. Having taken the required loyalty oath and completed the necessary paperwork for his release, he would now be free to leave.

Emmeline stepped forward, pulling an envelope from her reticule and offering it to Edward saying that it was from his sister Hattie. He took the envelope, removed the pages and, as he began to read them, Emmeline explained that she was the person to whom the letter was written and had come to take him to her home for a short respite during which time she would assist him in making arrangements to travel home to Mississippi. With that, she said no more, allowing Edward to finish reading and consider her offer. At first she feared that Edward would refuse her help. Instead he folded the letter, replaced it in the envelope and, nodding affirmatively, handed it back to her. Once back in the coach, Emmeline opened a basket in which she had packed a light box lunch thinking (correctly) that Edward would be hungry. Edward ate everything that was offered to him. He remained silent after that and dozed off for a time as the coach made its way south to Norfolk. The coach stopped first at the home of the Gatlings. Emmeline went in briefly, coming out with Isobel who had stayed with the Gatlings' housekeeper during their absence, making the acquaintance of their son Cassius for the first time, an event that would mark the start of a life-long friendship between the two.

THIRTEEN: "WAR DOES NOT DETERMINE WHO IS RIGHT – ONLY WHO IS LEFT."
~BERTRAND RUSSELL

Katie paused in her narrative and I thought that the weight of the story or exhaustion from the telling of it would cause her to delay continuing until the next day. She went to the little black lacquer casket, removed the key, and then opened Miss Isobel's traveling desk, just as Mr. Gatling had done previously. She lifted out a book with the word *Journal* embossed on its blue cloth cover under which were the initials "ER" in elegant but faded gilt script. Katie resumed her seat and paged through the journal obviously looking for a particular entry. In response to the look of confusion on my face, she explained. She was holding Emmeline Ricardo's journal, a personal record of her years in New Orleans with the Bentells, her time at Saint Mary's Hall, and the early years after her return to Norfolk with little Isobel. Rather than relying on her memory of the stories Miss Isobel had told her about Edward Sterling, she felt it best (and necessary) to consult the journal entries made while he stayed at the house in the summer of 1865. Katie said that in recent years, Miss Isobel had often read aloud from the journal in the evenings thus sharing the stories with her long-time companion. Katie confessed that during Miss Isobel's worsening illness, she had taken to reading passages from the journal to Miss Isobel as she lay in bed. That said, she resumed Edward's story referring to the journal entries as needed.

When Emmeline returned to the coach with Isobel, Edward's facial expression, up to that time resembling a stone wall obscuring all that was behind it, underwent a subtle change as the child sat down across from him. Isobel, still wary of strangers, particularly men, was torn between trepidation and an equally strong dose of curiosity about Edward. Emmeline saw that each of them was covertly (they thought) sizing up the other and wondered who would make the first move.

Isobel, a clever child, using her mother as a foil, asked if "the boy" was a soldier. Emmeline answered that he was but, the war thankfully being over, he was looking forward to returning to his family. Emmeline continued, telling Isobel that "Mr. Sterling" was going to be their houseguest for a while as preparations must be made for his long journey home. That said, Edward turned to Isobel and said she should call him by his Christian name rather than "Mr. Sterling" as long as that was acceptable to her mother. Isobel looked up at Emmeline for confirmation, which was given in the form of a nod. Isobel, no doubt wanting to show reciprocal generosity, announced that Edward could call her Isobel. For the first time, Edward's mouth turned slightly up and he said that he should like it if she would call him what his soldier brothers had, that being "Eddie." Not long after, he gave Isobel her own pet name: "Belle" and that is the only name he ever used for her thereafter.

Edward gradually ventured out from behind the wall that he had constructed to protect himself from the endless onslaught of pain and loss that had roiled his young life for years beginning with the death of his mother when he was but three years old. He had endless patience for his "Belle" and spent much of his time with her, playing games, taking walks, or reading to her. Emmeline could not help but notice the therapeutic effect each had on the other.

Edward told Isobel stories about his sisters Amanda and Hattie and life at their home in Mississippi where they lived with their Uncle William and his wife and their Aunt Clarissa, his mother's unmarried sister. Emmeline enjoyed hearing about her former students and encouraged Edward to share more family stories with her and Isobel. Edward talked about how his Aunt Clarissa had always spent her time doing two things: reading the Bible and doting on his sisters, brothers, and him. He smiled impishly when he told them how Aunt Clarissa had once found him reading Miss Ann Radcliffe's gothic mystery novel *The Romance of the Forest*, a book she described as wholly inappropriate for his Christian upbringing. Her devotion clearly meant a great deal to him.

Emmeline never dared ask Edward about his brothers' deaths or about his time at Point Lookout as a prisoner of war . . . but Isobel, in her innocence and curiosity, did ask questions. Her first inquiries were basic if broad: *What was it like to be a soldier? Was he afraid? Did he shoot anyone?*

Emmeline quickly moved to hush Isobel but Edward said it was "all right" and attempted to explain the realities of war to a child of not quite ten years old in terms appropriate to her age. Then, as if a thought had suddenly occurred to him, he rose and excused himself for a moment, returning with the threadbare and stained knapsack he had been carrying when they picked him up in Newport News. He reached inside it and removed a packet of what appeared to be letters fastened together with string. He untied the string and slowly looked through the letters selecting several and putting the others aside. Rather than reliving the horrors of his battlefield experiences by recounting those stories, he intended to share the content of those letters, believing that the sentiments and personal observations in them would transform newspaper images of charging horses, blazing guns, and battlefield victories into the actual essence of war: lives interrupted, families broken, plans usurped, ideals shaken, and faith stretched to its very limits.

Over the weeks Edward stayed with Emmeline and Isobel, he read selective portions of those letters to them. Among the letters were some written by Owen and Jessup Sterling to their sisters Amanda and Hattie who later forwarded them to Edward as mementos of their deceased brothers' affection for him. Edward also read from a letter to his father that he never posted. It seemed his way of articulating his conflicted feelings about the state of his young life and his sometimes fractious relationship with his father who he admitted often failed to reply to letters Edward sent him during the war. Emmeline, moved by what she heard and apparently with Edward's acquiescence, included what appeared to be transcriptions of excerpts of those readings in her daily journal entries. Katie said that Emmeline, from whom Miss Isobel had learned the power and beauty of written communication, had once thought to write a book composed of portions of wartime letters between soldiers and their loved ones as a means of capturing and illustrating the true cost and consequence of war. Listening to Katie read portions of letters written by the three Sterling brothers, I understood her meaning.

"The Regiment left last Sunday for Richmond and perhaps will get to Jamestown or Yorktown as well. I saw Owen on the 4th, he was quite ill again. Last Monday we had snow, sleet, and then rain and it kept on for three days without stop. The temperature was so low and the ground so wet, we were left no choice but to stay abed to avoid the freezing cold and damp. We left our beds of necessity only so long as to make and eat meals. When the sun finally returned, we were much relieved. The temperature had moderated as well where we were but looking up to the surrounding mountains, we saw them still blanketed in white." Jessup Sterling, Virginia, May 1862.

"I have had Edward detailed for my corps . . . I did not expect that he would enlist as he is not yet sixteen. I wrote that he might be sent home and said that I would provide a horse for his journey. Now that he will be sent to me, I will make it my responsibility to attend to his care and training as much as possible, considering his young age and what he will soon have to endure in service. Edward will use the horse I rode during the Battle of Seven Pines: a noble bay, of medium size, broad-chested and capable of great stride and speed. I have faith that Edward will be all right and a good soldier and I expect to do my part to make that so. The boy will become a man, have no fear or doubt." Jessup Sterling, Virginia, June 1862.

"My Darling Brother,
You probably can appreciate the anguish that weighs down my heart since I heard of the death of our dear brother – God knows I try to accept without question or complaint His will as we were taught that He only does right. I struggle with that and must suppress feelings that put me in conflict with our beliefs. No matter that, our Jessup is forever lost to us, a loss so painful that it leaves a hole in our hearts. We cannot again embrace him and no gnashing of teeth or bitter tears will change that. I am resigned to think of him as at peace and restored to our mother and sister who went before him.

I have not heard from you since I last saw you in Richmond and that causes me much concern. You must write as soon as you can and give me news of yourself, your health, conditions where you are camped, and about any contact you have had with General Sterling. I am anxious to know if you like our relation and if he has behaved warmly to you. You had better ask the General's advice about the disposal of Jessup's effects. If your present situation is better than you believe you would be if detailed with me, then my counsel is to remain there. But, if you believe otherwise, please waste no time in petitioning the General to transfer you to my regiment. I am certain, in light of Jessup's death, the General will understand such a request.

Brother, please avail yourself of all avenues to find out the specifics of Jessup's death and, most particularly where he was buried after he fell, whether separately or with others and recover and keep Jessup's sword if you may. May God bless you my dear brother." Owen Sterling, Virginia, September 1862.

Katie stopped reading and turned the open journal toward me pointing to the next few lines that were underlined for emphasis. I read those sentences, a form of explanatory note added by Emmeline with respect to Owen Sterling's request that Edward find out the particulars of their brother Jessup's death and burial: "It fell to Edward, the youngest of the three Sterling brothers, to seek out the places of death and burial of both his brothers, Jessup first and later Owen. He found Jessup's final resting place on the Manassas battlefield where he fell, a crude wood marker indicating his name. When Owen died in battle but a year later, Edward once again went in search of his fallen brother, confirming his burial near Fredericksburg."

As Katie resumed reading more excerpts from the journal, I wondered how Edward, a boy of fifteen when he went to war, endured so much pain and sorrow and what effect that had on the remainder of his life:

> "The scene in Fredericksburg left me heart-sick, so terrible was it there. Believing that the enemy would not again shell the city, residents who had evacuated as ordered made their return only to have shelling commence shortly thereafter. Women could be seen rushing through the streets in disarray screaming, wringing their hands, near pulling their hair out and calling out to us frantically to save them from the relentless enemy fire. Knowing no safe way to go, they were frozen on the streets, some with babes in arms, braving the danger in a courageous attempt to save their children's lives. Worse than their screams were the wails of their children, many barefoot with tears streaming down their young faces. The shells burst through the houses reducing furniture to shards, collapsing walls on our troops and igniting fires throughout the town.
>
> I performed my duties without injury, thank God, as shells flew by me. Our company attacked the enemy courageously and made them retreat from the bridge. We took cover in a nearby ravine where I saw one poor fellow whose face was all but gone and I was near a number of other wounded, some who had been but feet from me when hit. Seeing all this devastation, I could not help but think that even with all the privations at home, we must thank God that it is not worse or like it is here in Virginia where thousands have lost their homes to shells or by burning and fields that were once green and bountiful are wasted." Owen Sterling, Virginia, December 1862.

"I wish I could be with the family tonight. I see them at the supper table so fortunate to have an evening meal in times of such widespread want. Oh, how I long for the war to end, not only for the inestimable blessings arising from the dawn and return of peace, but so that I may continue toward my desired profession as a medical doctor without further disruption. Once graduated, I will hope to earn enough money to travel to London or Brussels to attend lectures . . . You may wonder that I am looking so far into the future but do not think me a dreamer or fool for doing so." Owen Sterling, Virginia, March 1863.

"Dear Father, I have not received any response from you to my recent letters but I trust you are not unwell, just perhaps occupied. I fear that, despite my protestations and explanations to the contrary, you may think me unequal to my brothers as to my commitment to the cause. I am no coward, although I have had questions about the validity of war as a means of resolving differences, particularly when the 'enemy' is, as in this case, an American brother. While I have no lack of personal or physical courage, I am conflicted morally. This is just the latest of such bouts of confliction as I have been visited by others in the last several years, those incidents leaving me struggling with a general aspect of sorrow and a mind not tranquil. I have been prey to my inner concerns and troubles and one of the reasons I turned to the army was to move on from that. It is strange that I am turning to war to dispel anguish and gloom and to make me a less isolated or callous person.

You may ask whence arose this inordinate trouble in one so young. Even if you do not ask, it is time that I told you my diagnosis. I am brought low by family differences, the issues and circumstances that divide our family and have done so almost since Mother and then my sister left this world. Am I the black sheep, the disappointment of the family? Perhaps if I left, it would be a relief to be rid of me. I recognize that I am not blameless in this and I continue to endeavor to mitigate my contribution to the situation that pains me.

I have learned from my recent experiences to value loyalty and fidelity and truth of heart above all the fickle earthly trappings that lure us from the true path to happiness. If the wickedness of the world could be brought to its knees, I would gladly slay it with one quick blow in the hope that its virtues would multiply in the place of its faults. While my life may remain obscure and unnoticed, I would be the happiest of men if I existed among those who had affection for me just the same." Edward Sterling, Virginia, October 1863.

Edward remained with Emmeline and Isobel for some six weeks during which time he put on much-needed weight and regained a reasonably healthy color. Emmeline was sorely tempted to encourage him to remain with them for an extended period as he had become so quickly a part of their small household. She knew that his family's fortunes were, like those of so many others, very reduced and their lovely home in need of restoration to make it near what it had been. He would be going back to Mississippi to face that and the reality that his brothers would never pass through the door of that home again. In the end, she relented from asking him to stay, thinking it unwise or selfish to interfere.

As the days counted down to his departure, Isobel became more sullen as she had become very attached to him. Emmeline tried, in vain, to soothe her by explaining how long it had been since Edward's family had seen him and how much they had been missing him . . . and he them. The parting was not easy for Edward either. He was deeply grateful for the hospitality Emmeline had shown him and he adored his Belle. On the day he left, he gave Isobel a bone carving he had made for her. It was a delicate rendering of a dove in flight. He told her that it had two meanings. First, the dove was a symbol of peace and, second, it was a reminder of the walks they took when they played a game to count all the birds they saw as they strolled. Isobel began to cry and said she had nothing to give him in return. Emmeline came to her rescue, handing Edward a carte de visite with a recent photograph of Isobel sitting on a delicately carved chair. He said it was the best gift he had ever been given.

Some weeks after Edward left Norfolk, a package arrived addressed to Emmeline. The sender was Hattie Sterling. Emmeline and Isobel unwrapped the package to find a copy of *The Scarlet Letter*. The enclosed note, from Hattie and her sister Amanda, thanked Emmeline so warmly for the help and the refuge she provided to Edward who had safely returned home to them. The note explained that the book had been given by then sixteen-year-old Jessup Sterling to his younger brother Owen in 1854 on the occasion of Owen's thirteenth birthday. Remembering how their former teacher had assigned that book as mandatory reading for her students at Saint Mary's Hall and how enthusiastically she discussed its themes and the author's purpose in writing it, they wanted her to have it as a measure of their affection and gratitude. Also enclosed, although never asked for by Emmeline, was a bank draft repaying the funds she had expended for Edward's expenses. Emmeline's initial reaction to the gift of the book was to send it back saying it was too precious a family possession to be given away. Isobel, whose latent precociousness was coming into bloom, said they *must* keep the book and only give it back if Edward himself came back to them to retrieve it. With that, the decision was made. The book became a prized memento of the Sterling sisters and Edward and had remained so for nearly a half century since.

Of course, I had questions for Katie, many questions, starting with what happened to Edward and did he and Miss Isobel ever see each other again. Katie, who had been hired by Miss Isobel about five years before her mother Emmeline's death in 1887, had periodically seen letters arrive from Edward Sterling and she had posted letters to him from Miss Isobel just as sporadically. She had noticed from the postmarks on Edward's letters that he moved around a good deal; letters were mailed in various states including Texas, Arkansas, and Tennessee and he apparently worked as a carpenter, a trade he learned when he returned to Mississippi after the war. She said she understood that Edward had visited Emmeline and Isobel on a few occasions when he was passing through Virginia, one of those visits happening just after she was hired by Miss Isobel. Over twenty years later and much to Katie's surprise, Miss Isobel one day asked her to post a note of condolence to Edward at an address in Arkansas as his wife had passed away. Apparently, not long after that visit to Norfolk when Katie met him, he had married an Albemarle County widow some dozen years his senior. As far as Katie knew, Edward was still alive, his last letter having arrived about a year past, mailed from Tennessee.

Amanda and Hattie Sterling's names were among those on Miss Isobel's list of people to be notified of her passing and word had been sent to them. Hattie, who had continued to correspond with Miss Isobel after Emmeline's death, had been aware of Miss Isobel's failing health. Edward Sterling's name had not been on the list, Katie believing that his current whereabouts were unknown to Miss Isobel and she thought to rely on his sisters to tell him of her passing.

FOURTEEN: "IF I MAINTAIN MY SILENCE ABOUT MY SECRET IT IS MY PRISONER...IF I LET IT SLIP FROM MY TONGUE, I AM ITS PRISONER."
-ARTHUR SCHOPENHAUER

While Katie and I were absorbed in matters of Miss Isobel's estate and the carrying out of her final wishes, Mrs. Boone often pitched in to help us. She also kept things in order at the house she shared with me and took responsibility for the children's reading program at the Library, including rounding up volunteers to replace me in that regard. She was, as always, faithful in every way possible, a source of quiet strength to all those in her orbit.

One afternoon several days after the funeral, she arrived at Miss Isobel's home in a more animated state than her usual. She had stopped by Miss Isobel's gravesite intending to leave a fresh bouquet of flowers there but, as she came up the cemetery path, she saw an elderly man crouched down in front of the grave, head bowed. As she got closer, she could see his lips moving but heard no words. Suddenly noticing her approach, he quickly laid down his own flowers on the grave, rose and moved away and up the path. She tried to follow after him and called out "excuse me sir" in an attempt to have him stop so she might speak to him. He neither responded nor turned to face her, and picked up his pace instead. Failing in her objective, Mrs. Boone reversed course and returned to Miss Isobel's grave. She bent down to see if the flowers had a card or note – there was none. It was then that she noticed something unusual. Rather than with a ribbon or string, the stems of the flowers were fastened together by what appeared to be a small cream-colored band of some kind. Upon closer examination, she saw that the band appeared to be a ring carved of ivory or bone and inset with small pieces of abalone. The carving consisted of two small hearts, one inset with that iridescent material and the other just hollowed out, no doubt having lost its abalone decoration somehow. To the left of the two hearts was carved the letter "E" and to the right of them, the letter "B." The ring was in very good condition but for the abalone inlay being missing from the one heart.

Katie and I had stopped all activity by that point and just as I was about to ask if she had removed the ring and brought it with her, she "confessed." Saying she had done "a most wicked thing," she said she had slid the flower stems free of the ring, retied them with a scrap of string taken from the flowers she had brought, and then put the ring in her pocket. With that, she reached into her pocket and produced the evidence of her transgression: the ring. As Katie and I excitedly took turns holding the ring, poor Mrs. Boone went on verbally lashing herself for what she had done. I asked Mrs. Boone to describe the "elderly" man and, when she was done, I was sure that he was the same man I had seen at the cemetery during Miss Isobel's funeral. More than that, after the prior evening's stories about Edward Sterling and his "Belle," I was convinced that the man was Edward and the initials on the carved bone ring signified their names. Katie was of the same mind.

I resolved to try and find Edward before he was once again "on the road." I enlisted Katie and Mrs. Boone to help me, the plan being to keep watch at the cemetery for his return to Miss Isobel's grave. We took turns at "cemetery watch" as often as possible over the next two weeks and I also spoke to the cemetery caretaker who promised to keep an eye out for the man in question. The "elderly man" was never seen again by any of us and no more flowers appeared mysteriously on Miss Isobel's grave. Having left what must have been a special token of his affection for her, he had vanished. Mrs. Boone continued to worry about what she had done in removing the ring from the grave. We resolved to speak to Mr. Gatling about what had happened and follow whatever advice he offered on that topic. For the time being, the little ring was safe in the black lacquer casket.

About two days later, Mr. Gatling asked that I come to his office to discuss one more aspect of Miss Isobel's will. I told him about Mrs. Boone finding the ring at the grave and about the man (Edward Sterling) who most certainly left it there and was also at the cemetery during the funeral. I could not tell from his facial expression how much (or how little) he knew about Edward

Sterling and Miss Isobel but imagined he must have heard about Emmeline's relationship with the Sterling family. He did not say anything about that but said that if I believed the ring was made by Edward as a token for Miss Isobel, I should consider keeping it and perhaps corresponding with Hattie Sterling (now Mrs. Hattie Noyes) to find out what, if anything, she might know about that. I said that I would be writing to Hattie anyway to offer to return their family copy of *The Scarlet Letter* to her. I could ask about the ring in the same letter.

With that discussion concluded, Mr. Gatling opened a folder and began to speak to me about a section of Miss Isobel's will that pertained to me personally. He read me a lovely passage that had been added as an addendum to her original will about a year earlier:

> "I, Isobel Aurora Verity, being of sound mind and desirous of ensuring that my final bequests and wishes be clear and capable of being efficiently and completely carried out, do declare this to be a Codicil to my Last Will and Testament dated June 14, 1908.
>
> To my dear ward, Grace Bridget Keane, I give, devise, and bequeath the sum of ten thousand dollars ($10,000) to be used for her continuing higher education in college, university, or other such institution or, in the alternative, as capital for her to start her own business enterprise. Should she wish to apportion said funds for use in pursuing both higher education and the establishment of a business, she may do so. In addition, it is also my direction that Grace

Bridget Keane receive my personal jewelry and only ask that, should she decide to sell said jewelry, she not sell the small carved dove brooch as that has special meaning to me and it is my desire that Grace should keep that as a reminder of my affection for her.

It has been said that 'happiness' cannot be pursued and captured but instead comes most often on the wings of incident or chance. Such was the unexpected serendipity that brought Grace into my way. Her youthful energy contagious, she gave me the gift of a brighter world lit by her curiosity. Despite having lost so much at such a young age, her spirit remained resilient, her eyes seeking the horizon optimistically. My dear Grace, the future is open to you, go out into the world with God's blessings."

Once again, I was left without words at Miss Isobel's generosity and I thanked God for putting me in her path at a time of such loss in my life. Her passing left me once again without "family," but the recent years spent under her care and guidance had brought me from an uncertain adolescence to the brink of a purposeful adulthood. I remembered imitating her in my bedroom mirror, anxious to develop the presence, confidence, and interpersonal expertise she exhibited. As much by example as by words, she had given me an invaluable view of the many aspects of womanhood. Now knowing that the accomplished woman that inspired me began her life as an orphan serendipitously rescued by three kind and courageous women during the war, I marveled at how far she had come from those dark days.

As I sat silent with my thoughts, Mr. Gatling spoke my name and I turned to him. He said there was "one more thing." Miss Isobel had left an envelope that was to be opened only in his and my presence. I saw what must be that envelope on his desk in front of him. He had been fingering it when I came into the office, putting it down when he began to read the Codicil document to me. He slowly broke the wax seal with Miss Isobel's initials that had secured the contents of the envelope and pulled out several sheets of paper. Neither of us knowing what to expect, he read the first few words aloud, paused and colored, that flush no doubt a reaction to the salutation of the letter that read "My dearest Cicero," that apparently being his middle name and a moniker only Miss Isobel had leave to use.

"My dearest Cicero,

As the old cliché says, if you are reading this letter, I am gone . . . and hopefully playing whist in God's blue heaven, my partner none other than our dear Lindy.

Let me begin by assuring you that Grace knows my family history. I have told her the story of how Emmeline Ricardo, her aunt Sarah Bentell, and her cousin by marriage, Mary Jane Verity Bentell, opened their hearts and their home to the orphan that was me, giving me shelter, food, and protection during the fraught years of the war. Mary Jane, every good thing that a mother should be but unable to bear any children of her own, made me her own child only to lose her life not long after. I was rescued once again by Emmeline Ricardo, in every way but birth my dear mother, who took me as her 'adopted' daughter and brought me with her to Norfolk so many decades ago. It is time to tell the full measure of my story, the part kept secret and known only to me, Mary Jane, Sarah, my mother and, later, Katie. Mary Jane, Sarah and my mother had taken that secret with them to their graves but my intent is to leave it behind me and open it to the light of day so that those who were so dear to me, in knowing it, can better understand the life I lived and the decisions I made. The telling will, I fear, take some time and I apologize for any excessive elucidation on my part as I attempt to set the out the events and characters of my tableau.

I will start by confirming that I was, for all intents and purposes, an orphan when I was taken in by the Bentell family. My first mother, my birth mother Aurora that is, was torn from me, never to be seen by me again. Based upon the violent circumstances of our separation, I can only think that she met a young death not long after. The man who fathered me was the one who quite literally tore her from me and then banished her to some place unknown to me then or now. Lest you think he did so to protect me or with any motivation of love for me, I tell you he did not love me or even like me. He had some perverse curiosity about me, the reason for that I will soon tell you. I did live in his house, if my status in that house could be called *living*.

The house, once a fine old mansion, had something in common with its owner, both descending into wreck and ruin as the years went by. An unhappy and cruel man, he only inherited the house and surrounding properties due to the premature death of his older and more decent brother. He assumed control of the family legacy and still miserable with himself, used some of his new wealth to buy all manner of alcohol and spirits that he used as 'medicine' for his ills, mental and physical. An alcoholic faux aristocrat, he ran the small, once successful plantation into the ground and himself along with it. From time to time he took in parasites who claimed to be relatives and it was my role, from about the age of five, to play servant to him and them.

My mother was mostly forbidden to enter the house and lived in a small cabin on the grounds with others of her family. I expect the picture is becoming clear to you: my mother was one of my father's slaves and, in fact, so was I. Many a story has been told of 'masters' taking advantage, often brutally, of their female slaves and this is such a story. My mother was not more than sixteen when she became pregnant with me. That my life came at the cost of her innocence and likely led to her death, has haunted me. When I was taken from my mother and moved from the cabin to the big house, my mother, then about twenty, protested . . . and begged that I be left with her. I was offered a handful of candies and was told there would be more at the house. Not understanding what was happening, I waved to my mother as if I would be back shortly. Once at the house, the reality of things quickly became clear. My mother tried repeatedly to see me despite being beaten when caught. I was told that if I did not 'behave' and do as I was told, she would be beaten again because of me. I vowed to do nothing to bring punishment to my mother and I began an existence that was not unlike the girl in the Brothers Grimm story of Cinderella; I washed, cleaned, fetched and more for people in that house who, by blood, were supposedly my own relations.

My mother made a plan to escape her captivity along with me and, not surprisingly, it failed. I thought he would kill her right then but he did not, only promising that we would never, ever, see each other again "except in hell." I never did see her again after that night. Some people said she was sold to another plantation owner but others whispered that she had killed herself and her body was then disposed of. Either way she was, from that day forward, "dead" to me.

My father's drinking got ever worse, he slept very little and raged very often. I think in some way he missed my mother as I sometimes caught him staring at me as if deep in thought. About two years after my mother disappeared, when I was about seven, I risked all by asking him what had become of my mother. Drunk as usual, he threw down his glass, shattering it on the flagstone and staggered in my direction. I backed up but not far enough. He swung at me and the back of his hand struck my forehead hurling me to the ground. I felt the warm, salty taste of liquid at the corner of my mouth and touched my throbbing forehead. His large signet ring had sliced open my skin near the hairline. He offered no help nor did his *cousins* who saw what had happened. I ran to the kitchen and the cook, also a slave, gave me a rag wet with cool water and told me to push down on the cut until the bleeding stopped. She also gave me a salve of some kind that eventually helped the wound to heal.

I did not ask about my mother again and I vowed to run away. The war that brought sorrow and devastation to so many proved to be the means of my escape. My father had nearly drank himself to death and no longer had the strength or awareness to keep track of my movements. Then the Union naval forces sailed into New Orleans and slaves began to claim their freedom. One day I made to go to the well and just kept walking . . . well, running, from that place. Not long after, I saw some mothers and children clustered near a cart where three women were giving out bread, milk, and some other provisions. I stood and waited among them. It was there that I met Mary Jane Bentell and my life was changed forever.

By now you should be asking yourself a question: since I am 'white,' was my mother Aurora also white? No, my birth mother was a beautiful Negro girl, her skin a warm cashew beige. It is more than likely that she or a parent of hers was also fathered by a white man but I have no knowledge of that. By whatever circumstance, I was born 'white' by skin color but not by bloodline.

With this letter you will find a carte de visite with a photograph taken in New Orleans in about 1863. It is a grouping of five light-skinned children and the caption underneath the photograph reads: 'Slave Children of New Orleans.' Notice the girl on the right with the wavy dark hair; if you look closely – you may need a magnifying glass – you will see a scar on her forehead near the hairline. Yes, that child, then known by her birth name, Mariah, was me. These photographic cards, printed and circulated in the North, were sold for one dollar to raise funds to underwrite schools for freed slave children, the thought being that the sight of light-skinned or 'white' slave children would have more appeal in garnering donations.

I once saw another such card showing the photograph of a very austere middle-aged woman who posed with another of the 'white' slave children, a girl of about ten. The caption proclaimed 'Redeemed in Virginia by Catherine Latimer' (the dour-faced lady) and further stated that the child, named Rosa, had been baptized by Henry Ward Beecher in Brooklyn, New York. I remember asking my new mother Emmeline what the card said, unable to yet read. She told me and I asked if I too had been 'redeemed' . . . by her. I never forgot her answer. She said that she was certain that I had done nothing in my young life that warranted redemption and suspected that neither had little Rosa. She then took that card and threw it into the hearth where it soon fell to ash.

My new mother gave me both a new home in Norfolk and a new name: Isobel Aurora Verity, my middle name a respectful reminder of the young woman who gave me life, and I have been Isobel for a half-century now. I am not sure how the decision was made to leave my Negro heritage behind in New Orleans but I can say, without doubt, that concealing it afforded me opportunities and advantages that the truth would have denied me. I am sure of one thing, however, any decisions my mother Emmeline made were prompted by her sincere desire to do her best on my behalf. And so, I became what I seemed to the eye: white.

My new mother continued to teach and tutor me as she had in New Orleans and I was hungry to learn. Besides my letters and numbers, she instructed me in history and geography to ready me for school. She told me that my birth mother's family had come from a place called Africa, far across the ocean. I asked if someday I might go there and she said that perhaps we would go together and also visit the place where her family had once lived as it was also across the same ocean. That was when I first heard about the Ricardo family's roots in Spain. Much later I understood that they had been prosperous Sephardic Jews living first in Spain and later in Amsterdam before coming to America and settling in Charleston.

After those early years, the circumstances of my birth and my mixed race were rarely brought up between my mother and me but neither were those facts forgotten by either of us. As my mother had predicted to Frederick Bentell, 'the disruptions of war' gave cover to our secret. The Norfolk that we returned to was a quite different place than she had left so many years before. The population had become a mix of natives and new residents who had come from other parts of the country during the war and made the decision to stay thus setting off changes in culture, viewpoints, and future direction for the city.

As for the two of us, we went on, formed a life as mother and daughter, and things took their new natural course as we, like the newcomers, blended into the 'new' post-war Norfolk. I wondered from time to time about my birth mother and the family I knew nothing about. As I became a grown woman, I grasped more completely how my life had started and what it might have been had I not broken free from my father and veered off the dirt road that was my life and onto the pavement of New Orleans that delivered me to my second mother Emmeline.

The inevitable day came when my mother sat me down to talk about my future in a particular sense. She had detected, dear Cicero, that you were 'sweet' on me and foresaw the possibility of my returning your affection. Therein presented a biological fact that must be faced. If I were to consider marrying, I must disclose my past to my future husband both for the sake of honesty and because of the chance that I would bear a child with brown skin. I had never been one of those girls who dreamt of her future wedding, picturing herself at the altar with the love of her life and adorned in a gorgeous dress. My dreams, both day and night versions, turned more to the possibilities I learned from books that made me imagine going to foreign lands or having a profession not traditionally thought of for women. My mother and I were a set, like salt and pepper – no pun intended. I really could not see myself leaving her to take on another partner. So, my friend, I feigned ignorance to your overtures but resolved to keep you as my dearest friend no matter what I had to do. That task got easier when I realized how much in love Lindy was with you and how happy you two could be together.

Only once more in my life did I face the same dilemma . . . with Edward Sterling. I was, in the beginning, his curious little sister of sorts, eight years his junior and just a child when he came to us at the end of the war. Over the ensuing years, he visited us several times as I was growing up and into adulthood. I had become attached to Edward so easily as a child and, no matter how much time passed between his visits, our connection was revived immediately upon seeing him again. When I was in my late twenties, he came to us again and, for the first time, our relationship showed signs of blossoming into something new. We both felt it. One night he made a proposal of marriage and I almost said yes; the word was all but formed on my lips but then reality came back to me as clear as day and I told him I could not accept. I made the excuse that I was needed by my mother and would never leave her to marry. Edward countered by saying we could all live together. I told him our life was ordered in such a way that we could not alter it to include a third person, even one we were both so fond of as he. He left us and I did not hear from him for a long time, my refusal of his proposal causing a rift that was ever painful to me. When he did write, he told me that he had married a few years after he last visited us and his wife was a Virginia widow from Albemarle County. I must admit that I did wonder what my life might have been if I had married but I knew I had done the right thing for the two men I had loved."

FIFTEEN: *"SHALL WE NEVER GET RID OF THIS PAST? IT LIES UPON THE PRESENT LIKE A GIANT'S DEAD BODY."*
-NATHANIEL HAWTHORNE
(THE HOUSE OF THE SEVEN GABLES)

Mr. Gatling paused, looking spent, and put down the remaining pages of Miss Isobel's letter. He suggested that we go down the street for a bite to eat and then return to read the rest of what she had written. I agreed. Very little was said over our meal, both of us overwhelmed. What could one say after hearing such an incredible and unexpected revelation? It would take time, a lot of time, to take it all in and understand it in the context of the person we knew before and the totality of the woman we now knew for the first time. After our short respite, we returned to the office and Mr. Gatling continued reading:

"When my mother Emmeline died, my thoughts returned quite intensely to my birth mother Aurora and my biological family. I became convinced that I should go to New Orleans and try to locate some vestige of that family. By that time, all my New Orleans Bentell relations were deceased but for my mother's cousin Virgil, the notable maritime newspaper reporter and columnist. Although Virgil had many contacts that could have been valuable in my search, the Bentell men had never known my true origins and there was no sense to open that door then. Virgil died about three years later and, hearing of his passing, I revived my plan to go back to New Orleans. I took Katie with me although I did not tell her the truth about why we were making the journey.

I concocted a story that I was a distant relation of the man who was actually my birth father as, under no circumstances, would I claim that brute as the man who fathered me. The old mansion was in uninhabitable ruins, the property grown over and gone to seed. The once-proud house was a withered pile of rotting timber, stripped of all its material accoutrements long ago by scavengers and the desperate.

I ascertained, however, that some of the former slaves who had been bound to him and that property remained in the area, some of them actually still occupying the old ramshackle cabins. I steeled myself and walked out on the property to those cabins. I spoke to several of the inhabitants asking about people (slaves) whose names I could remember from my childhood with no success.

I asked what had become of the master of the house and, dare I say it, was thrilled to learn that he had died not long after my escape. Drunk as usual, he staggered out onto the second story porch bellowing for one of the servants to come to him with more alcohol. As he leaned over the railing, it gave way (likely due to his failure to do even the most essential maintenance on the property) and he was thrown to the ground, a dissipated, broken heap. Ironically, with his just death, his direct family line went extinct . . . but for me.

As I was preparing to leave the property, a woman of about fifty or so came forward to me. She said she remembered Aurora and her little girl Mariah as she and Aurora had grown up together. I asked if she knew what had become of Aurora. She cast her eyes down and said that the 'master' had come out to the cabin one night in a drunken rage and had choked her to death. Her body was dragged away and some people said her corpse had been thrown down the well. I thought immediately of the ruse I had used to escape from the big house . . . that I was going to the well . . . and my stomach turned over. She also told me that Aurora's family left the property as soon as they could after the fall of New Orleans to the Union forces. The trail was cold and I knew I would never find my Negro family. Before leaving, I went to the well. My eyes filled with tears as I said a prayer for my first mother who loved me so well that she lost her life as a consequence.

Years later, I told Katie the real reason we went to New Orleans and, until this letter, she has been the only person I ever told that truth. I thought never to tell her, my belief being that sharing such a secret is akin to putting a yoke on the other person and making them share the shouldering of the burden you had been carrying on your own. Then, one evening a dozen or so years ago, a little too much brandy after dinner loosed lips, mine and Katie's both. She became contemplative and suddenly blurted out the confession that she was "a fugitive." Taking a deep breath and exhaling it with a sigh, she said it was time she told me about her past.

Catherine Ferry (that was the name her parents gave her) was born into a poor farming family in the rural west of Ireland in 1865. (I always remember that as Katie and I both began a new life that year, she as a babe in her mother's arms and me as the adopted daughter of Emmeline Ricardo.) She was one of seven children, and the youngest of them, born to her parents as an unexpected "late in life" arrival. The family's existence was eked out on a small tract of land leased from a local English aristocrat she called Lord "Something or the Other," his name mattering not except as the person who could, without justification or notice, dispossess them at any time. Although the potato blight and resulting Great Famine had been over for a decade, potatoes and poverty were still the themes of daily life for families like the Ferrys.

Katie's siblings grew to adulthood (except for two girls who died in childhood), married, and set about eking out their own existence, helping their parents when they could. By the time Katie was twelve, both of her parents had died . . . or as she described it: "had worn out their mortal shells in the relentless struggle for the next crop and the next rent payment due the landlord." Katie's oldest sister, Delia, took her in and for some months she lived with Delia, her husband Patrick, and their four young children.

Katie saw the strain her presence put on the meager amounts of food available to Delia and her family and, feeling guilty, thought she would seek out employment as a washwoman or servant in the nearby town. She went from shop to shop and to the local inn asking for work with no success. Exhausted and hungry, she stole the end of a small loaf of bread as she left the inn and once in the street pulled it from her pocket and began devouring it. Suddenly she felt a hand grip her arm from behind. Whirled around, she found herself facing the innkeeper's wife who tore the bread from her hand and dragged her back to the inn. The constable was sent for and, adrenalin surging through her veins, Katie yanked free of the innkeeper's wife and bolted out into the street. Afraid to go home lest she lead the constable or the innkeeper to her sister's family and perhaps give their landlord a reason to evict them, she fled and never returned home again.

She walked from one small town to another, asking for paid work or offering to work in exchange for food or shelter. Eventually she put aside enough to buy passage in steerage on a ship headed to America. At the age of thirteen, Catherine Ferry, fugitive from the law, left Ireland, never to return to her homeland and family. She became one of thousands of young Irish girls and women who arrived here and became servants and housemaids, that profession eventually bringing her to Norfolk and to my mother and me.

I asked Katie if she ever sent a letter to her sister Delia to explain what had happened. The answer was "no." Her shame would not allow it. They were better off without her.

Katie's secret revealed and the brandy glasses once again refilled, I responded to her honesty with a large dose of my own and, as of that evening, the yoke of secrecy bound us together, a bond that proved no small gift of relief to both of us."

The remainder of Miss Isobel's letter was less a continuation of the story as, for the most part, the story had been told and instead read more like a "confession." As jarring and candid as the first part of the letter had been, the second half was heartbreaking.

It revealed the personal demons that stalked her: her struggle with her identity, her feelings of dishonesty in keeping her secret from even those closest to her, and her life as what she called an "imposter." She wrote about how the trip to New Orleans after her mother died was an attempt to reconnect with her real roots but, even in doing so, she questioned her motives and resolve. She wondered if she had found Aurora or some others of her Negro family, would she really have had the courage to unmask herself or would she have lost her nerve and retreated from them. In any event, being once again "alone in the world" was a crossroads for her and the first time in her life that she alone would decide who she was. No longer the "master's slave daughter" or the "war orphan adoptee," she was simply Isobel . . . or Mariah . . . or some mix of both of them that defied labeling.

When the road back to Mariah ended with her peering down into a well that was very probably her mother Aurora's grave, that journey abruptly ended. There would be no relatives to meet, no memories sad or happy to share, no years to catch up on, no plans to make for the future. It was then she faced the reality that she was a branch severed from a family tree that was later cut down, the remains of its roots left to wither and die. Her branch had then been grafted to her second mother's own ancestral tree, that tree now having lost all of its leaves to death. There would be no family reunions in her future. Standing at the intersection of those family crossroads she only saw dead-ends in every direction. The decision was essentially made for her: she was and would be

Isobel to everyone in her world . . . Katie later being the only exception.

They say that if a lie is told often enough, it essentially becomes truth in the mind of the one who has told it repeatedly. Miss Isobel said that was never the case for her, particularly once her mother died. What had been their shared secret, their joint burden, and the very basic bond of their life together was suddenly transferred lock, stock, and barrel to survivor of the two of them, that being no small load to lift up and carry forward.

At the bottom of the final page of the letter, just above Miss Isobel's signature, was written the following quotation attributed to John Churton Collins, essayist, lecturer, and noteworthy 19th century English professor of literature: "If we knew each other's secrets, what comforts we should find." There was also a short post-script on the reverse of that page that simply said: "It is understandable that you may have questions about what I have revealed to you. Please do not hesitate to speak with Katie as she may be able to help you. In fact, I encourage you both to talk with her as it will be good for her to have someone to talk to about these things after so many years of keeping my secret."

We did talk to Katie in the days following our reading of the letter that Miss Isobel had left for us and she was most definitely right. Katie was able to give further clarity and context to the revelations but, as importantly, it was plainly evident that talking with us was cathartic for her. One of my questions was about Emmeline Ricardo's journal. I asked Katie what Miss Isobel had instructed be done with that fascinating book. She smiled and said there was a "story" related to that intriguing volume. Among Emmeline's final instructions to be carried out upon her death was that her daughter Isobel destroy that journal. Miss Isobel, in her early thirties at the time of her mother's death, suddenly found herself looking to the horizon. Seeing the approaching crossroads awaiting her, she made the first decision of her new independent life: she would not destroy the journal. Its pages were her pages as much as her mother's and she might very well need the information on those pages as she faced the biggest dilemmas and decisions of her life. As for now, with Miss Isobel's death, all the key players in its pages, with the possible exception of Edward Sterling, were dead and its text could bring no harm to them. Katie said that it would be my and Mr. Gatling's decision to keep or destroy the journal. My immediate but unspoken reaction was that it should not be destroyed and I hoped that I might get the chance to read every page of it.

With everything that had happened I had completely forgotten about the generous bequest Miss Isobel had left for me to underwrite my education or the establishment of my own business. It looked like I also had a lot of decisions to make in my new "independent" life, those decisions being so strikingly different than the ones that faced Miss Isobel so long ago. I stopped by Mr. Gatling's office a few days later, my intent being two things: first, to tell him that I had been looking into local two-year colleges where I could continue my education and, second, to speak with him about allowing me to keep the journal with the promise that I would neither show it to or discuss its contents with anyone.

I pulled open the door to his offices, entered and came to an abrupt halt at the sight of Andrew Pritchard sitting behind the desk where I had first seen him over eighteen months earlier. Catching sight of me, he quickly stood up. He looked thinner than I remembered and there were gray shadows under his pale blue eyes. We greeted each other with polite awkwardness and I passed into Mr. Gatling's private office. I restrained myself from asking about Andrew and began to speak about my plan to continue my education at a two-year college. I explained that the Aitchison Institute (in Norfolk) offered coursework of the kind I was seeking and had recently embarked on a cooperative agreement with the College of William and Mary in Williamsburg that would bring teachers from that storied school to Norfolk to present lectures to the student body of the Institute. Tuition fees were moderate, I would be able to remain living at home and, as such, Miss Isobel's bequest would more than cover the cost of my two-year attendance.

Mr. Gatling, availing himself of the short pause when I ceased speaking to take a needed breath, said it sounded like a fine plan and he only had one question: just what was the coursework I intended to pursue? I had an answer for that question readily at hand. I explained that I would be taking classes that would prepare me for a career as a writer and journalist, my interest born of the influence of Miss Isobel in concert with my own predilection for reading and books. Although he most certainly understood my meaning even from that short statement, I went on to mention what the Library had brought to my life, not the least of it Miss Isobel herself. And then there was the effect and impact of Miss Isobel's eloquent letter that Mr. Gatling and I had shared, her words painting vivid images and joining her heart and soul to ours. With that said, I smoothly segued to the subject of Emmeline's journal, making my plea on that count with all the force of purpose I could muster.

Mr. Gatling, somewhat accustomed to me by now, inhaled, lifted his head as he did and then slowly exhaled as he nodded. He said he was very pleased that I would be continuing my education but my objective of becoming a writer and journalist came as quite a surprise to him. He thought I might take a position at the Library or continue school to become a teacher or even establish myself as a bookseller. He cautioned me that female journalists were, for the most part, a rarity, and going down that road would present any number of obstacles. As for being a "writer," he said that aspiration could be pursued in my "free time" even if I did become a librarian, a teacher, or a bookseller.

While I was thinking that Miss Isobel would not like to hear such counsel coming from her dearest friend, Mr. Gatling resumed speaking. Having given me what he characterized as "the appropriate and perfunctory caution about my journalistic aspirations," he stated that he was ready to offer me his personal support and encouragement for that endeavor just the same. There was the man Miss Isobel loved so well. As for Emmeline's journal, he said I should, from that day forward, consider it mine.

As I rose to leave, I almost forgot to ask about Andrew Pritchard's apparent return to his employ. Mr. Gatling said that Andrew's return was precipitated by unhappy circumstances that had befallen him. Andrew, who with his deceased younger sister had been given refuge at the Roanoke orphanage, received his education through the efforts of that institution, the plan being for him to become the bookkeeper of the orphanage upon the retirement of the incumbent who had been in that position for decades. Mr. Gatling, acquainted with a gentleman who was a benefactor of the orphanage, was contacted by that man almost two years earlier and asked to provide Andrew with an apprenticeship as the last step of his education. Mr. Gatling kindly agreed to do so and Andrew arrived in Norfolk not long after, that being just weeks before I had graduated from school and returned to Norfolk myself. Several months later, the apprenticeship completed, Andrew returned to Roanoke to assume his new position and also to be married to a fellow resident of the orphanage named Ophelia.

Mr. Gatling said that Ophelia had been an angel of mercy during the illness of Andrew's sister. Andrew and Ophelia leaned heavily on each other during those awful days and in their mutual grief when the young girl died. From that shared sorrow and friendship somehow arose a plan for them to marry, each only having the other it seemed. Mr. Gatling said that the gentleman from the orphanage had concerns that the basis of the marriage was solace, consolation, or even a sense of duty on Andrew's part but hoped he was mistaken in that regard. The marriage took place as planned, Andrew became the new bookkeeper, and it appeared that the young couple finally had prospects for happiness. Several months after the marriage, Ophelia began exhibiting symptoms of the dreaded disease that had taken Andrew's sister. Andrew was laid very low by the thought that Ophelia had contracted tuberculosis as the result of her tireless efforts on behalf of his sister. Their fears were later multiplied by the news that Ophelia was with child. Ultimately, both wife and child were lost when Ophelia succumbed to consumption, apparently just days after Miss Isobel had done the same.

Mr. Gatling was once again contacted by the gentleman associated with the orphanage who told him the whole terrible story and again asked for help on Andrew's behalf. Andrew had determined to leave his position and the place that was a daily torturous reminder of all he had lost. Mr. Gatling was asked if he might have a position that Andrew could fill, the gentleman recommending him highly and thinking that placing him with Mr. Gatling would benefit Andrew by having him with people he already knew . . . and who knew what had happened to him. Mr. Gatling, whether or not he actually had an open position, readily agreed to take him on and so it was that Andrew had recently arrived again in Norfolk.

My mind traveled back to that day at Catawba when I unexpectedly ran into Andrew who was pushing Ophelia in a wheelchair.   My surprise at seeing him and, moreover, the debilitation of his wife, was turned to pity when I bent over her to say "good day" as I parted from them and saw her bone-thin hands resting protectively on the small bulge that told me she was pregnant.

When I left Mr. Gatling's office, Andrew was not at his desk, having been sent on an errand for one of the accountants.   I was relieved as I had no idea in the world what I should say to him had he been there.

SIXTEEN: "TO MITIGATE ANOTHER'S GRIEF IS TO ALLEVIATE OR DISPEL ONE'S OWN."
-TRYON EDWARDS

When I next saw Mrs. Boone, I told her about having found Andrew in Mr. Gatling's office. When I saw no expression of surprise on her face, I guessed that she already knew he was returned and working for Mr. Gatling and I realized that I was not the only one who could keep a secret.

Andrew, having warm feelings for Mrs. Boone who had welcomed him and fed him during his apprenticeship, had sent her a note to tell her he would be returning to Norfolk and did reveal something of the circumstances surrounding that. She knew he was widowed and well-understood his desire to remove himself from a place that was a constant reminder of those he had lost. No one need explain that to her.

I asked her why she had not told me about Andrew's return and her answer was the stuff of her usual concern for me. With Miss Isobel's passing still so at the forefront of heart and mind and knowing my conflicted feelings about my prior infatuation with Andrew, she felt the news of his move to Norfolk could wait as she believed he would not arrive for several weeks. In fact, she was not aware that he had arrived and was already working for Mr. Gatling.

She said she hoped I held no ill will toward him as she felt sure he had meant me no injury and, even if his behavior had lacked in some aspect of propriety, he deserved a second chance to go along with his new start in life. As usual, I could hardly have found any grounds for disagreeing with her reasoning. It would be a new start all the way around. I no longer suffered from any romantic fantasies about Andrew nor did I harbor any "ill will." In fact, now on the brink of my twentieth birthday, I was no longer a giddy schoolgirl, that creature replaced by a woman about to step off into an exciting and yet-to-be-discovered future brimming over with possibilities.

Mrs. Boone's succinct and sage counsel laid the trail to a measured but ultimately very satisfactory reconnection between Andrew Pritchard and me. In our first encounter before his marriage, if he ever had any reciprocal feelings for me like those I imagined I had for him, I do not know and have no desire to find out. Upon his return, we became friends, very comfortable and at ease in each other's company, our new connection not unlike the bond that developed between Mr. Gatling and Miss Isobel. He was often to supper with us at the house and took us out occasionally as well. Sometimes we did walk out together, just the two of us, going to the cinema or some local event or just strolling through town. We talked about being the last of our respective families to walk this earth, shared stories the other had not heard, and reminisced about the people we had lost . . . except for one of those he never ever spoke of: his lost child. I feared his silence on that point was the effect of some sense of guilt that held his tongue and left him to mourn alone as punishment for having escaped the tuberculosis that took Ophelia and their baby. I thought how guilt, like a secret, has a corrosive effect on the heart and soul.

Of course Andrew was not the only one keeping secrets. I would never speak to him of Miss Isobel's story or Emmeline's precious journal. Even as we walked together as friends, our secrets kept us separate, and so, apart. I wondered if either Andrew or I would ever marry in the future, each of us so rooted in our "aloneness" and singularity for so much of our young lives. I felt certain that while our commonality of loss would always be a bond between us, it would never join us together in marital life.

The closing of Miss Isobel's estate was rapidly approaching and I expected her home to be put up for sale only to find out that her instructions were for it to be converted to studio space for local artists and artisans, the ownership of the building and its renovation to be under the direction of the Norfolk Arts Association. I wondered if Katie would stay in Norfolk or use her pension bequest to purchase a small home elsewhere . . . or even to travel home to Ireland. When I noticed partially packed boxes at the house, I asked and was delighted to hear she would be remaining in Norfolk. Rather than retiring (she was a little young for a rocking chair), she would be moving to Mr. Gatling's house to replace his elderly cook who was quite ready for that rocker.

I had made it very clear to Mrs. Boone that I expected, rather insisted, that she and I remain housemates. Knowing I was sincere and wanted that for my own sake as well as hers, she made no resistance. Everyone settled, it was time for me to prepare for the new school year. Also, in imitation of Mr. Gatling who got his first banking job by confidently convincing the bank manager to give him an unpaid trial position, I had boldly entered the offices of two local newspapers and proposed to write and submit articles for their publications without compensation. I reasoned that as I was attending classes at the Institute, I could also be writing those articles in the hope of seeing them published and as a means of promoting myself as a candidate for a paid position in the future.

That plan hatched, I invited Mrs. Boone, Katie, and Andrew to accompany me to the Monticello Hotel for a lecture being presented by Mrs. Lila Meade Valentine, a Richmond-born activist in causes including female suffrage, equal education for all children in Virginia regardless of race or economic status, and healthcare reform. A founding member of the Richmond Education Association, the Instructive Visiting Nurse Association and the Equal Suffrage League of Virginia, she was the epitome of modern womanhood to me. Mustering more of that boldness of mine, I contacted the Equal Suffrage League and asked to interview Mrs. Valentine during her stop in Norfolk. Mrs. Valentine, although more than "busy," agreed to a short talk immediately preceding her lecture. Notebook and pencil firmly in hand and armed with a series of questions I had prepared, I arrived twenty minutes early. Mrs. Valentine graciously answered as many as she could before time ran out. Her lecture was glorious, articulate, and inspiring and I scribbled as fast as I could to take down excerpts to use in my article including the following:

> "If I were asked to give one reason above all others for advocating the enfranchisement of women, I should unhesitatingly reply: the necessity for the complete development of woman as a prerequisite for the highest development of the human race.
>
> Just so long as woman remains under guardianship, as if she were a minor or an incompetent – just so long as she passively accepts at the hands of men conditions, usages, laws, as if they were the decrees of Providence; just so long as she is deprived of the educative responsibilities of self-government – by just so much does she fall short of complete development as a human being, and by just so much does she retard the progress of the race.
>
> And so it comes to pass that the suffrage movement with all that it implies of freedom for self-development and equality of opportunity, is a clarion call to the woman of today.
>
> In rapidly increasing numbers, forward-looking men are welcoming the new woman in whom they find, beyond the wife and mother known to them, a comrade capable of fully taking her place beside him. Indeed it goes without saying that men and women together are bringing to pass the new order of things; so that instead of this movement creating gender antagonism as some are prophesying, we see emerging a clearer understanding of the need of man for woman and a

closer cooperation in their work both in and out of the home."

I wrote, rewrote, edited, revised, tore up and restarted my article about Mrs. Valentine for hours . . . and days in fact . . . until I felt I could not do better with it. I delivered it to the editors of the two newspapers, one tossing it to the side of his desk while telling me that it was "stale" as three days had passed and the speech had already been given all the coverage it was going to get. The editor of the second newspaper gave it a quick scan and said he would have his assistant editor for "women's interest pieces" look it over. Ultimately, it was published on the women's page, albeit it having been cut substantially in the process. That one small victory was all I needed to be sure of my career decision.

And so, dear reader, our journey together is nearing its end as the stories of Miss Isobel and all of us whose paths touched, crossed, joined with or diverted her own have been amply told for now. I am preparing now to attend to one last loose end, that related to the Sterling brothers' copy of *The Scarlet Letter*. Quite by accident, it recently came to my knowledge that the widow of General Malcolm Sterling, the revered distant cousin of those young Sterling men, had taken up residence in Norfolk in recent years. Like Miss Isobel, Mrs. Boone, and Andrew Pritchard, her relocation here was the result of a family loss: that of her daughter Charlotte who died in childbirth. Upon that tragic event, the General's widow, Maude Sterling, moved to Norfolk to live with her son-in-law and assist in the care and upbringing of her grandchildren. Mrs. Sterling, not far from being eighty years old, lost her soldier husband when she was but twenty-eight and had honored his memory by wearing black ever since.

With Mr. Gatling's intercession, I arranged an appointment to visit with that great lady, my intent two-fold. First, I will tell her about Jessup and Owen Sterling, her husband's relations, who also lost their young lives in the war but were inordinately proud of their familial connection to the General. I will bring with me the copy of *The Scarlet Letter* that one brother had given the other as a birthday gift and show her the inscription. Assuming our conversation goes well and she is agreeable and up to it, I then intend to ask if I might interview her as to her thoughts and reminiscences in light of the upcoming fiftieth anniversary of the General's death on a battlefield near Richmond in 1864. I gave Mr. Gatling my promise to show Mrs. Sterling the utmost courtesy and consideration in speaking with her and to exert no pressure on her to accommodate my request.

After speaking with Mrs. Sterling, whether or not it results in an interview and my writing an article, I will send the Sterling copy of *The Scarlet Letter* to Hattie Sterling Noyes so that she might pass it down to her children who I am sure she has told about her brave soldier brothers. I had thought it a most queer thing that sixteen-year-old Jessup Sterling gave a copy of *The Scarlet Letter* to his brother Owen as a thirteenth birthday gift. With all the books that Jessup might have chosen for his brother, Dumas's *The Three Musketeers* or Defoe's *Robinson Crusoe* for example, I wondered why he would select *The Scarlet Letter*, a book whose central character is a disgraced young woman in Massachusetts. My curiosity even had me planning to ask Hattie for her recollections on that point . . . until I recalled what Edward had told Emmeline and young Isobel about his doting, Bible-reading Aunt Clarissa and her reaction to finding him reading a "wholly inappropriate" gothic mystery novel. I feel sure that *The Scarlet Letter's* didactic and cautionary tale of sin, sinners, punishment, and redemption would have been much more to her liking and suspect she had a hand in its selection as a birthday gift for Owen.

As for the small carved bone and abalone ring I still believe was left at Miss Isobel's grave by Edward Sterling, Hattie wrote to say that I should keep it. Since Miss Isobel had left me the bone brooch that Edward had made for her, Hattie felt that the two should remain together. She said that she had written to Edward twice, first to tell him of Miss Isobel's illness and later to share the sad news of her death. Both letters were sent to the last address she had for Edward (in Tennessee) and while neither was returned as "undeliverable," she had received no response from Edward either time. For my part, I am very pleased to be able to keep that little ring. Foolish or not, I still hold out some small hope that Edward will return and that I will discover him one day at Miss Isobel's grave. He will not flee, we will talk at great length about Miss Isobel, and then I will ask *his* permission to keep the ring.

EPILOGUE: *"WE ARE THE CHILDREN OF OUR MOTHERS AS WELL AS OUR FATHERS. WE INHERIT THE DEFECTS AS WELL AS THE PERFECTIONS OF BOTH."*
-LILA MEADE VALENTINE

I can hardly believe it has been nearly three years since Miss Isobel's death. I am now an honors graduate of the Aitchison Institute having studied in the areas of creative writing, literature, and journalism. While I was still a student, one of our local newspapers did the unimaginable and hired a female staff reporter named Fanny Cahill. She had "cut her teeth" as an underling at a larger newspaper in New York and with dogged perseverance and sharp elbows had made her way into the newsroom over a period of years during which time people said she had spent many a day (and night) among her male counterparts in smoky rooms, saloons, and police precincts. Tiring of that environment and having made something of a name for herself, she decided to try the avenue of being a "large fish in a small pond" for a change and found her way to our city. Her arrival in Norfolk was the subject of much talk and curiosity, her red hair and bright green eyes naturally adding to the interest.

I considered her arrival the opening of the door to my own future. In fact, I recently applied for a position as Miss Cahill's "assistant" and I am hopeful that, with my education and having had a few of my uncompensated articles published, I will get that job. If not, my contingency plan is to enlist Miss Cahill as a mentor, pitch my articles to her for her feedback and, hopefully, win her recommendation that my work be published.

While a cliché, all indications are that the world *is* changing. In fact, it never stops changing but we only seem to notice the changes that resonate with us or affect our plans and expectations. I, for instance, look forward to casting my first vote as an enfranchised citizen of this country and think that day will soon arrive. At the same time, I look ahead with dread as another war looms upon the horizon, this one likely to send American boys a world away to fight and die in places where they do not even comprehend the language of their enemies. General Robert E. Lee, the epitome of a warrior, once wrote:

> "What a cruel thing is war: to separate and destroy families and friends, and mar the purest joys and happiness God has granted us in this world; to fill our hearts with hatred instead of love for our neighbors, and to devastate the fair face of this beautiful world."

Still, humanity (particularly the male portion of it), remains deaf and blind to such wisdom despite it being proven time and time again through bitter first-hand experience that the underlying causes of war are rarely honorable and almost always base: greed, jealousy, the pursuit of power, or all of those.

In my musings about writing an acclaimed novel or a great work of non-fiction, I am ever aware of the ready inspiration that presents itself in the everyday lives of people who go mostly unnoticed as they navigate from day to day in pursuit of life's basic necessities or in response to unexpected challenges that befall them. In their stories we find the full gamut of emotions and experiences and see humanity at its best . . . and worst. Even if I were a writer with a great creative gift, I would be hard-pressed to invent a more interesting or compelling story than those chiseled out by real people journeying down the road of life. In support of that premise, I only need submit the lives of Isobel Verity, the Bentells, and the Sterling brothers or even dear Katie as evidence.

I frequently wear the carved dove brooch made by Edward Sterling and left to me by Miss Isobel and, wanting to make certain I did not lose it, had the jeweler replace the old clasp with a safety catch. I *always* wear the carved bone and abalone ring left on Miss Isobel's grave. I had also shown that to the jeweler and inquired about replacing the abalone inlay missing from one of the two hearts but then decided not to do so. Why? My flights of fancy interpreted the missing abalone as symbolic of Edward Sterling's heart, left "empty" by Miss Isobel's refusal of his marriage proposal. Too small for my finger, the ring hangs around my neck on a delicate silver chain, hidden from the sight of others under my clothing. Still hopeful that I will meet Edward Sterling one day, I keep the ring at hand, and will do so as long as I believe that the boundaries of his likely life expectancy leave a chance that he is still alive.

I have often thought about Miss Isobel's love for *The Scarlet Letter* and, not long after her passing, finally finished reading the copy she had given me as a gift. Over time I thought I began to understand her attachment to Hawthorne's tragic story of love, secrets, revenge, and redemption and particularly to Hester Prynne, the stoic keeper of the secret that first tenuously underpinned four lives and eventually undid two of them. I imagined myself as both Hester and Miss Isobel in turn. I remembered Miss Isobel's wide-eyed but speechless reaction to Mrs. Ward calling Hester Prynne a "fornicator." Eventually I came to my own interpretation of what the story meant to Miss Isobel and how it informed her assessment of herself, a realization that pained me.

To Miss Isobel, Hester Prynne was more than Hawthorne's well-formed multifaceted heroine. She was an ideal. Alone, she carried the weight and bore the consequences of two secrets, each belonging to a man who, for all intents and purposes, had abandoned her rather than expose himself. There was a time when I assumed Miss Isobel identified with Hester in that both of them lived under the shadow of secrets. Slowly rereading the letter Miss Isobel left for Mr. Gatling and me, I focused on the passages in which she talked about feeling dishonest and an imposter due to the secrets she concealed from even those most close to her. She judged herself harshly in life and, finally, in death, purged herself in what she seemed to think a much overdue admission of her sins and acknowledgement of her guilt. Assuming that to be her view, she would have identified not with Hester Prynne but instead with Hester's beloved, irresolute partner in sin, the Reverend Arthur Dimmesdale who, upon the throes of death, revealed his own part in that sin's commission and concealment. In truth, Arthur Dimmesdale bore the weight of his secret, albeit covertly, every day without exception as, no doubt, Isobel Aurora Verity bore the weight of hers. Her dear Hawthorne said it thus: "What other dungeon is so dark as one's own heart! What jailer so inexorable as one's self!"

I recalled, once again, the scene when Miss Isobel died. She had opened her eyes one last time, raised her extended arms slightly above the quilt that covered her and said just one last word: "Mama." Which mother she was reaching out to I cannot say but I choose to believe that she saw Aurora and Emmeline, and perhaps Mary Jane, waiting together to wrap her in their arms and, earthly burdens left behind, she found both family and peace restored to her.

"No language can express the power, and beauty, and heroism, and majesty of a mother's love. It shrinks not where man cowers, and grows stronger where man faints, and over wastes of worldly fortunes sends the radiance of its quenchless fidelity like a star."

~Edwin Hubbell Chapin

CPSIA information can be obtained at www.ICGtesting.com
Printed in the USA
LVOW06s2239020915

452563LV00011B/153/P